THE 30-DAY WHOLE FOOD COOKBOOK FOR BEGINNERS

Revitalize Your Life With 1100+ Days of No-Fuss, Wholesome Recipes to Boost Family Health and Enhance Energy. Master Whole30 With the 30-Day Meal Plan

Vivian Harrow

TABLE OF CONTENTS

CHAPTER 7: MAIN COURSES FEATURING RED MEAT 57

CHAPTER 8: DISHES FEATURING PORK 67

CHAPTER 9: POULTRY DISHES 77

CHAPTER 10: SEAFOOD AND FISH RECIPES 87

INTRODUCTION

Embarking on a journey towards better health and vitality can often feel like preparing for a long voyage — it requires preparation, dedication, and a solid plan. That's where the Whole30 diet steps in, not just as a dietary regimen, but as a transformative lifestyle that rejuvenates your body and spirit. This book, particularly designed for those at the threshold of their Whole30 journey, aims to simplify what might initially seem a daunting path. The Whole30 diet is more than a mere elimination protocol. It's a pledge to purge your meals of processed foods, sugars, dairy, and grains that often leave you feeling sluggish and spent. Instead, it welcomes wholesome, nutrient-packed foods that are as close to their natural state as possible—foods that heal, nourish, and refresh. From busy parents who strive to set up a nourishing meal plan for their family, to young professionals seeking solace in a healthy lifestyle amid their hectic schedules, the reasons to start Whole30 vary. However, the benefits converge at a common point—enhanced health, sharper mental clarity, and boundless energy. This introduction sets the stage, not just to inform, but to inspire and guide you through the practical aspects of Whole30, and to share the transformative potential it holds.

By turning these pages, you commit to exploring how everyday ingredients can be transformed into exciting and revitalizing meals. We will delve into the philosophy and science behind the Whole30, revealing why each step is vital and how it contributes to your overall well-being.

Prepare to embrace a month of undeniable transformation where you won't merely change what you eat, but you'll change how you think about food. Let's begin this journey of discovery together, unveiling not just recipes, but a new horizon of health and vitality waiting to be realized.

OVERVIEW OF THE WHOLE30 DIET

When we consider refining our lifestyle choices, particularly our diet, the breadth of information available can be overwhelming. Yet, among the myriad of eating plans and health advice, the Whole30 diet emerges—a beacon for those seeking to reset their eating habits and catalyze a true change in their health.

The Whole30, designed as a 30-day nutritional reset, is more than a diet; it's a dedicated philosophy towards consuming whole foods. Created with the aim to systematically pull you away from processed goods and sketchy labels, it enjoins you to embrace foods in their simplest forms—fruits, vegetables, quality meats, seafood, and nuts—eliminating sugars, grains, dairy, legumes, and anything that threatens your well-being.

Understanding the need for such dramatic changes begins with grasping the fact that our bodies sometimes react poorly to certain food groups, whether it's the bloating discomfort from dairy or the spike-and-crash episodes driven by refined sugars. These reactions are not always immediate, nor are they always evident. Symptoms such as chronic fatigue, skin irritations, or persistent digestive issues are often signals drowned out by the noise of everyday health advice.

Whole30's primary goal is to clear that noise. By stripping down your diet to the basics for 30 days, the program challenges you to listen to your body without the usual interference. This isn't about counting calories or aiming for weight loss—though those might occur—it's about identifying foods that truly nourish you and those that don't.

Why only 30 days, you might wonder? The answer lies in the simplicity of habit formation. Research suggests that it takes about a month to form a new dietary habit—long enough to notice a significant impact, but short enough to remain achievable. The set timeframe serves as a manageable yet meaningful period to experience visible and palpable changes in one's health and energy levels.

During these 30 days, you'll likely face challenges as your body adjusts to this new mode of nourishment. The initial phase might bring about a sense of withdrawal, particularly from sugar and processed foods, which are ingeniously designed to be addictive. This is where the Whole30's strict, no-compromise approach kicks in; it does not allow for subtle slips or gray areas, which are often present in other diets. It's this black-and-white approach that fosters a clear understanding of how specific foods affect you—after reintroduction, you'll find it easier to discern which foods keep you vibrant and full of energy, and which drag you down.

Reintroducing the eliminated foods one at a time after the 30-day mark is as crucial as the elimination phase itself. This stage is investigative, a deep dive into personal nutrition. How you react to reintroducing dairy or grains can be incredibly telling. A slight headache, a return of the afternoon slump, or a resurgence of digestive discomfort can pinpoint sensitivities you never knew you had.

One might conclude that Whole30 sounds demanding—and indeed, it requires commitment. Yet, the transformations reported by many who have embraced Whole30 speak volumes. Beyond just notable physical improvements—clearer skin, reduced inflammation, and often weight loss—participants recount enhanced mental clarity, improved sleeping patterns, and a newfound awareness of their eating behaviors.

Imagine each meal being a step towards understanding your body better. For thirty days, you indulge in a cycle of learning and healing, nurturing yourself with meals that replenish and energies that last. You'll learn not only to look at a label but to understand what goes into your body and how it affects your day-to-day life.

Preparing for Whole30 involves mental readiness and physical preparation. Clearing your pantry is just the start; preparing your mind for the journey is equally crucial. Expect the resistance, from both your habitual reaches for a comforting sweet or from well-meaning friends who find your new diet "restrictive." Herein lies the challenge and beauty of Whole30—it demands full engagement and promises substantial rewards.

Thus, the Whole30 diet isn't merely a monthly planner of meals but a journey towards self-discovery and lasting health improvement. It's a testing ground to recalibrate your relationship with food, crafted thoughtfully to break the autopilot of unhealthy eating habits and reconstruct a framework that supports, nourishes, and revitalizes.

To embark on this journey, consider this not as giving up on variety or flavor but as stepping away from hidden toxins and stepping closer to optimal health. With every compliant meal, you're rewarded not just with a sense of accomplishment but with a building block towards a healthier life—a life where food is both the source of pleasure and the foundation of good health.

THE SIGNIFICANCE OF COOKING WITH WHOLE FOODS

In a world where convenience often overtakes quality, making a conscious decision to cook with whole foods is a profound shift back to the roots of what our bodies truly need. The significance of this shift is not merely about dieting—it is about fostering a deep connection with food, understanding its origins, and appreciating the processes that bring it to our tables.

Cooking with whole foods is both a philosophy and a practice that encourages the use of ingredients in their most natural or minimally processed state. Think fresh tomatoes plucked from the vine, vibrant carrots pulled from the earth, and grains that whisper the story of the fields they grew in. These are foods that have not been stripped of their nutrients or flavor; they are robust, rich, and resonating with life's vitality.

The shift towards whole foods is a response to the increasingly processed nature of many diets globally, where convenience often results in meals laden with preservatives, artificial flavors, and added sugars. This way of eating, while quick, can disconnect us from the natural tastes and nutritional benefits of food. Whole foods, in contrast, offer a tapestry of benefits, key among them being the robust array of nutrients they deliver.

When foods are processed, they often lose essential vitamins, minerals, and fibers. A grain, once whole, when refined into flour, loses its bran and germ—the parts richest in nutrients and fiber. This is just one example of how processing can dilute the nutritional value of food. By choosing whole foods, one naturally sways towards a nutritionally dense diet. It is not just about adding years to life but adding life to your years through improved health.

Moreover, whole foods possess inherent properties that can help regulate the body's natural rhythms. For instance, the natural fiber in plant-based foods helps slow the absorption of sugars, controlling blood sugar spikes and contributing to a steady energy supply throughout the day. Imagine enjoying a meal that lifts your energy levels, brightens your mind, and fills you with vitality. This is the daily reality of a diet centered on whole foods.

The environmental impact of choosing whole foods over processed alternatives is also noteworthy. Less processing means fewer resources expended in the form of electricity, water, and packaging materials. This, in turn, means a smaller environmental footprint per meal. If one considers this impact cumulatively, over months and years, the choice of engaging in a whole foods-based diet emerges not just as a personal health choice, but as an act of environmental stewardship.

Another crucial aspect of cooking with whole foods is the flavor. Once you start to engage with the true tastes of whole ingredients, your palate undergoes a renaissance. You begin to notice nuances in different tomato varieties, the slight sweetness in fresh peas, and the earthy richness of whole grains. This journey through flavors can reinvent meal times, turning them into an exploration of sensory delight.

Cooking becomes a joyful exploration rather than a mundane task. Each meal is an opportunity to experiment with textures, colors, and flavors. Creating dishes from scratch allows one to tweak meals to personal taste preferences while also prioritizing health. This could mean bringing out the natural sweetness in foods with a slow roast, or using herbs and spices to heighten sensory experiences without the crutch of added sugars or excessive salt.

Yet another dimension of using whole foods is the cultivation of community and culture. From farmers' markets to community-supported agriculture (CSA), seeking out whole, local foods connects you with a network of growers and producers passionate about quality food. This connection not only supports local economies but also builds a community around the shared values of health, sustainability, and well-being.

Thus, the decision to incorporate whole foods into one's diet is multifaceted. It promotes a healthier, more sustainable way of living, not only in the physical sense but in a broader socio-economic context as well. It's a step toward reclaiming autonomy over one's health, one meal at a time, fostering a greater appreciation for the natural world, and the body's natural healing abilities.

The narrative of whole foods is not one of deprivation but one of celebration—a celebration of nature's variety, of the intense flavors and textures available to us, and the joy of creating meals that are as nutritious as they are delightful. In embracing whole foods, we embrace a life where food becomes more than just fuel—it becomes a source of healing, joy, and unification.

As we move forward in this book, remember that each choice for a whole ingredient over a processed one is a step toward better health and a more vibrant life. It's not just about changing what's on your plate; it's about transforming your life, one meal at a time.

12

Embarking on the Whole30 diet is akin to setting out on a refreshing journey toward improved health and vitality. This chapter is your comprehensive guide to understanding the essentials of the Whole30 diet—a program that has revolutionized how many of us think about food and its impact on our bodies and minds.

At its core, Whole30 is more than just a dietary regimen; it's a month-long clean-eating plan designed to reset your eating habits, reduce harmful cravings, and heal your digestive system by eliminating foods that are known to cause adverse health effects. The promise of Whole30 lies in its simplicity and the profound effect it can have on your body's functioning.

Why Whole30, you might ask? Imagine feeling more energetic, noticing clearer skin, or even alleviating some of those nagging aches and pains that you've accepted as part of your daily life—all through the food you eat. This diet emphasizes whole, unprocessed foods, which means each meal is packed with nutrients essential for robust health.

Often, people feel intimidated by the idea of eliminating sugar, grains, dairy, and legumes. But think of it not as a restriction, but as an exploration of new flavors, textures, and combinations. You'll discover how satisfying and flavorful meals can be when they focus on natural ingredients.

As we delve deeper into the operational mechanisms of the Whole30 program in this chapter, you'll gain insights into why certain foods are excluded and how others can foster a better balance within. Understanding these principles is crucial, as it arms you with the knowledge to make informed decisions about what you eat—decisions that align with your health goals.

Whole30 isn't just about changing what you eat for 30 days; it's about starting a journey toward lasting wellness. It teaches you to listen to your body and to understand its responses to different foods. This program is your stepping stone to a life where food is both nourishing and enjoyable—a way to revitalize your body and your life.

EXPLAINING THE WHOLE30 DIET

The Whole30 diet emerged from a transformative idea: that the food we eat significantly impacts every aspect of our health. This dietary program is not just a fad or a temporary fix; it's a purposeful path designed to reset your body's chemical responses and alter your relationship with food.

Launched in 2009 by Dallas Hartwig and Melissa Hartwig Urban, Whole30 is structured as a strict elimination diet that spans 30 days. The primary aim is to identify foods that might be having a negative impact on your individual health—physically, mentally, and emotionally. Many swear by the noticeable differences they experience, be it increased energy, clearer skin, reduced digestive issues, or even relief from chronic pain.

The Core Philosophy

The philosophy behind Whole30 is straightforward yet profound: by removing certain food groups from your diet for 30 days, you give your body a chance to recover from whatever ill effects those foods may be causing. After this period, foods are gradually reintroduced one at a time, allowing you to observe how your body reacts to each. This process helps pinpoint allergies, sensitivities, or just general adverse effects associated with specific foods.

Foods to Eliminate

During the Whole30, several food groups are completely eliminated. These include:

Sugar and Artificial Sweeteners: Whole30 requires a complete purge of all forms of added sugar and sweeteners, whether it's white sugar, honey, maple syrup, or artificial sweeteners like aspartame. The idea is to curb sugar cravings and dependencies.

Alcohol: Given its effect on the liver and overall metabolism, alcohol is strictly off-limits during these 30 days.

Grains: This includes all grains like wheat, rice, barley, and corn. The rationale here is that grains are seen as a potential irritant to the gut, and they might contribute to inflammation.

Legumes: Beans, lentils, peanuts, and soy are also excluded due to their potential to affect digestive health and hormonal balance.

Dairy: Often implicated in digestive problems and skin issues, all dairy products are eliminated to assess their impact on the body.

The Foods to Embrace

Rather than focusing solely on restrictions, Whole30 heavily promotes the consumption of whole, unprocessed foods:

Vegetables: A cornerstone of the diet, vegetables are rich in nutrients and fiber, essential for good health.

Fruits: Whole fruits are encouraged for their nutrients, though in moderation due to their natural sugars.

Meat and Seafood: Quality protein sources like grass-fed beef, pork, poultry, and seafood are emphasized.

Eggs: Packed with protein and other essential nutrients, eggs are a staple in the Whole30 meal plan.

Nuts and Seeds: These are great sources of healthy fats and proteins (excluding peanuts, which are classified as legumes).

The Aim of Whole30

Whole30's ultimate aim is not weight loss—it's about health, vitality, and well-being. Weight loss might occur as a side effect, but the primary goal is to foster a healthier relationship with food and to better understand how different foods affect your body and mind.

The Challenge of Whole30

It's not just about changing what you eat—it's about changing your habits and behaviors around food. This includes learning to read labels meticulously, preparing more meals at home, and becoming acutely aware of how foods affect you emotionally, psychologically, and physically.

For many, the challenge lies in staying disciplined, especially when faced with social events or routine disruptions. It's a test of willpower and dedication but offers a reward in the form of profound personal insights.

Reintroduction Phase

After the 30-day elimination phase, a structured reintroduction phase helps you systematically re-assess your tolerance to the previously eliminated food groups. Each group is reintroduced individually over a few days while observing symptoms and reactions. This critical phase helps create a personalized eating plan that optimally supports your individual health.

Potential Benefits

Adherents often report transformative effects. These can range from improved energy levels and sleep patterns to a reduction in chronic pain, clearer skin, and better digestion. More importantly, it promises an enhanced awareness of how food affects your mood and physical feeling, encouraging a more mindful way of eating.

Whole30 as a Learning Tool

Beyond its structure, Whole30 can be seen as an educational tool. It equips you with the knowledge to make better food choices, understand nutritional content, and appreciate the benefits of foods in their whole, unprocessed form. It's about gaining a new perspective and using this knowledge to sustain a healthier lifestyle even after the initial 30 days.

Whole30 is not just about what you exclude but what you include, and through this inclusion, discovering a diet that is uniquely suited to your body and your health needs. It's a journey of self-discovery, a shift towards mindful eating, and, above all, a passage to better health. Each step taken with Whole30 helps pave the way toward understanding your body and the food that fuels it, setting a foundation for a lifetime of healthy habits.

ADVANTAGES OF THE WHOLE30 DIET FOR HEALTH

Imagine waking up feeling refreshed, your body lighter and full of energy — that's the transformative promise of the Whole30 diet. Rooted in the philosophy of elimination and reintroduction, this diet offers multiple health benefits that go beyond superficial changes to foster deep, lasting impacts on overall well-being.

Rejuvenated Physical Health

The most immediate advantage reported by many who embrace the Whole30 diet is a noticeable improvement in physical health. The diet encourages a heavy intake of vegetables and fruits, which are loaded with vitamins, minerals, and antioxidants that help reduce inflammation — a root cause of many chronic diseases. By eliminating processed foods and sugars, the body is less burdened by unhealthy fats and preservatives, leading to better cardiovascular health and reduced risk of chronic conditions like Type 2 diabetes and hypertension.

Enhanced Digestive Functioning

Digestive health sees a significant boost on the Whole30 program. Removing grains, dairy, and legumes — which can be difficult for some people to digest — helps mitigate symptoms of bloating, gas, and irregular bowel movements. As the gut heals from the irritations caused by these foods, nutrient absorption improves, leading to better overall health and an increase in energy levels. This can be particularly life-changing for those suffering from digestive disorders such as irritable bowel syndrome (IBS) or inflammatory bowel disease (IBD).

Mental Clarity and Improved Mood

The elimination of sugar swings and additives found in processed foods also means more stable blood sugar levels, which has a profound impact on mental clarity and mood stability. The diet's emphasis on whole foods ensures a steady supply of energy that prevents the mid-afternoon slump many experience. Moreover, omega-3 fatty acids from increased seafood consumption and antioxidants from fresh vegetables and fruits can enhance cognitive functions and may help in reducing symptoms of depression and anxiety.

Strengthened Immune System

A diet rich in diverse nutrients strengthens the immune system. Whole30's emphasis on quality protein sources, fresh produce, and healthy fats provides the body with essential building blocks for immune cells. As the body detoxes from additives and sugars, its ability to fight off infections and inflammation improves. Additionally, the reduction in gut inflammation supports a healthier microbiota, which plays a crucial role in immune function.

Long-term Eating Habits

Whole30 not only impacts one's health during the 30 days but also teaches invaluable lessons about food and its effects, lessons that many carry into their lifelong eating habits. The reintroduction phase is particularly educational as it helps individuals understand which foods work best for their bodies. This awareness fosters a more mindful approach to eating and empowers people to make choices that support their health long-term.

Improved Relationship with Food

Transitioning to Whole30 can change one's emotional and psychological relationship with food. Many report a decrease in food cravings, especially for sweets and processed foods, as they begin to appreciate and savor the natural flavors in whole foods. This dietary shift can also lead to a decrease in compulsive eating behaviors and a healthier approach to using food as nourishment rather than comfort.

Better Skin and Appearance

The benefits of Whole30 can also be seen on the outside. The diet's high intake of fruits, vegetables, and healthy fats leads to better hydration and intake of nutrients essential for skin health. Many participants notice clearer, more glowing skin after the 30 days, thanks to the exclusion of sugar and dairy, which are often culprits in skin issues such as acne and eczema.

Hormonal Balance

For those struggling with hormonal imbalances, Whole30 offers an opportunity to reset. Foods rich in processed sugars and unhealthy fats can wreak havoc on hormones. By focusing on balanced meals with adequate protein, fats, and carbohydrates from whole foods, the diet can help stabilize hormonal levels, which is especially beneficial for conditions like Polycystic Ovary Syndrome (PCOS), thyroid issues, and adrenal fatigue.

Sustainable Weight Management

While weight loss is not the primary focus of Whole30, many participants do lose weight due to the elimination of calorie-dense, nutrient-poor foods. More importantly, the diet promotes a healthier way of managing weight in the long term without counting calories — a liberty that many find liberating.

Increased Energy Levels

Finally, the synergy of all these health benefits is often manifested in the form of higher, more stable energy levels. Freed from processing the additives and sugars in junk food, the body becomes more efficient in its metabolic processes. Simultaneously, improved sleep patterns, a common benefit of the Whole30 diet, contribute to a feeling of vitality.

Like turning the keys to a finely-tuned machine, Whole30 opens the door to a multidimensional enhancement of health. By stepping away from foods that hinder our health and focusing intensely on those that promote it, this diet not only revamps our meals but reinvigorates our life's vigor — a whole renewal from the inside out.

OPERATIONAL MECHANISM OF THE WHOLE30 PROGRAM

At its heart, the operational mechanism of the Whole30 program is grounded in a structured yet flexible approach designed to reset your nutritional habits and reshape your relationship with food. This mechanism is not merely about what you eat; it's about redefining how you think about food on a fundamental level.

The Reset Phase

The first and most critical component of the Whole30 program is the 30-day reset. During this phase, you eliminate foods that are potentially damaging to your health. This is not arbitrary; the foods chosen for elimination include those commonly linked to systemic inflammation, digestive issues, and chronic health conditions. These include grains, sugars, dairy, legumes, and alcohol.

The rationale behind this is deeply rooted in nutritional science. For instance, removing sugar eliminates a quick source of energy that the body uses before it taps into fats. The absence of grains and legumes helps address issues like bloating and dietary discomfort, and dairy is often removed to test for lactose intolerance or dairy sensitivities that might manifest as skin issues or digestive upset.

The Reintroduction Phase

Following the 30 days of elimination, the next pivotal part of the Whole30's operational mechanism is the reintroduction phase. This phase is as critical as the reset; it's the process through which you reintroduce the eliminated foods one group at a time, carefully observing how your body responds. This stage is designed to be highly personalized. For example, you might reintroduce dairy for a day and then return to the Whole30 baseline for two days, monitoring any changes in energy, mood, digestion, or other potential symptoms.

This methodology turns your diet into a personalized experiment where you can clearly see which foods your body tolerates well and which it doesn't. It empowers you to make informed decisions about your diet that go beyond following trends or generalized diet advice.

Behavioral Change Through Structure

A significant part of the Whole30 program's effectiveness lies in its structured approach to changing eating behaviors. By having a clear set of rules and a defined time frame, it's less about perpetual restriction and more about learning and exploration within a safe, controlled framework. This structure is crucial because it challenges but doesn't overwhelm, thereby encouraging compliance and facilitating real, observable changes in dietary habits and health.

Psychological Reconditioning

The Whole30 isn't just a physical detoxification process; it's a psychological reconditioning regarding how you view food and nutrition. It teaches mindfulness in eating—encouraging you to think about the flavors, the source of your food, and its effects on your body. This increased awareness is a cognitive shift away from eating simply to satisfy hunger or cravings, moving instead toward an understanding of food as nourishment.

Community and Support

Another operational mechanism that enhances the effectiveness of the Whole30 program is its community support aspect. Participants are encouraged to connect with others who are also on the diet through various platforms, from forums and social media groups to official Whole30 coaching sessions. This community provides a network of motivation, advice, and empathetic support, all of which are crucial for navigating a challenging month of dietary changes and can significantly impact one's success on the program.

Flexibility within Guidelines

Despite its strict rules, Whole30 does offer flexibility. This flexibility is not about the food choices—which remain constant during the elimination phase—but about tailoring the diet to individual lifestyles and needs. For example, athletes or those with higher physical demands can adjust their intake of Whole30-compliant carbohydrates to suit their energy requirements.

The Whole30 program operates on a clear, well-structured yet adaptable framework designed to navigate the complex nature of individual health and nutrition. It functions effectively at multiple levels—from the biochemical impacts of food elimination to the psychological impacts of dietary change and community support. Each aspect is meticulously designed to work synergistically, providing a comprehensive approach to improve health, reset dietary habits, and enhance life quality. Through this structured yet personally adaptable approach, participants embark on more than just a dietary change; they start a transformative journey to lasting health and wellness.

DIETARY DOS AND DON'TS ON THE WHOLE30 DIET

Embarking on the Whole30 journey is like setting the sails for a voyage across uncharted nutritional waters. It challenges your conventional eating habits and seeks to redefine your approach to food. To guide this transformational journey, understanding the dos and don'ts of the Whole30 diet is crucial. These guidelines act not only as your compass but also as a map to help you navigate your way through the dietary changes, ensuring you reap the full benefits while avoiding potential pitfalls.

The Dos: Foundations of Success

Do Focus on Whole, Unprocessed Foods: At the heart of Whole30 is the commitment to eating whole, unprocessed foods. This means your diet should predominantly consist of fresh vegetables, fruits, meats, seafood, nuts, seeds, and certain healthy fats. These foods are packed with the nutrients needed to support your body's healing and health optimization processes.

Do Plan Your Meals: Success on the Whole30 is heavily reliant on effective meal planning. Without a plan, you are more likely to fall back into old habits. Spend some time each week to plan your meals, ensuring you have the ingredients on hand. This foresight removes the stress of deciding what to eat every day and helps you stay committed.

Do Read Labels Carefully: Many foods, especially packaged ones, contain hidden non-compliant ingredients such as sugars, soy, and food additives. Reading labels is crucial to avoid accidentally consuming something that could hinder your progress.

Do Hydrate Adequately: Hydration plays a vital role in flushing toxins and keeping your body's systems functioning optimally. Ensure you drink plenty of water throughout the day, which not only supports detoxification but also helps curb hunger and maintain energy levels.

Do Listen to Your Body: Understand that everyone's experience with Whole30 is unique. Listen to your body's signals and adjust portions or meal timings if needed to suit your specific health needs and lifestyle.

Do Seek Support: Whether it's from friends, family, or online communities, having a support system can greatly enhance your motivation and commitment. Sharing your journey with others provides emotional encouragement and practical tips that make navigating the Whole30 more manageable and enjoyable.

The Don'ts: Avoiding Common Missteps

Don't Replicate Junk Food with Compliant Ingredients: One of the core principles of Whole30 is to change your food behaviors and eradicate cravings, not just to substitute ingredients so that you can continue eating non-nutritive foods. Creating paleo pancakes or cookies, even if they're made with Whole30-compliant ingredients, can undermine the spirit of the program.

Don't Ignore Portion Sizes: While Whole30 isn't about counting calories, ignoring portion sizes can lead to overeating. The goal is to eat until you are satisfied, not stuffed. It helps to be mindful of the balance of proteins, fats, and carbohydrates on your plate, which can guide you to better satiety and nutrition.

Don't Skimp on Planning: If you fail to plan, you plan to fail. This adage is particularly true for Whole30, where impulsive eating choices can lead to setbacks. Planning not only involves meal preparation but also foreseeing challenging scenarios, such as dining out or attending social events.

Don't Disregard Reintroduction: The reintroduction phase is as significant as the elimination phase. Slowly reintroducing food groups and observing your body's reactions helps you understand which foods support your health and which do not. Skipping this step can negate some of the insightful benefits of the entire program.

Don't Get Discouraged by Challenges: You might face days when the diet feels particularly challenging, or you might accidentally consume something non-compliant. It's important not to get discouraged. Acknowledge the slip, learn from it, and continue your journey. Persistence is key to experiencing the transformative effects of Whole30.

Through understanding and adhering to these dietary dos and don'ts, you cultivate not only a disciplined approach to eating but also a profound connection with food. This connection allows you to make choices that honor your body's needs, leading to sustainable health and well-being long after the 30 days are over. The rules guiding the Whole30 diet aren't just about restriction; they are stepping stones to a revitalized life, making every mindful meal a building block towards lasting health.

CHAPTER 2: PLANNING AND PREPARATION

Embarking on the Whole30 journey can seem daunting at first—navigating through a whirlwind of rules, grocery lists, and the daunting fear of facing the unknown culinary challenges. However, the secret weapon to mastering this transformative experience lies not just within willpower but within thoughtful, strategic planning and preparation.

Think of your Whole30 journey like setting out on a month-long expedition. You wouldn't start a long hike without a map and some preparation; similarly, delving into Whole30 requires equipping yourself with the right tools and knowledge. This chapter is your preparation guide, ensuring you're not just surviving your dietary quest, but thriving throughout it.

The starting point is understanding the full significance of the meals you'll be preparing. Each recipe isn't just about adhering to a list of dietary dos and don'ts; rather, it's about creating a foundation for longer-term healthy habits that nourish both the body and the soul. Adopting Whole30 can be a fresh start, a way to reset your body's dietary clock. Thus, how you plan and what you prepare has a profound effect on your success.

Let's consider meal prep as an essential building block. Preparing your meals in advance can drastically decrease daily decision fatigue and avoid the temptation of off-plan choices. By having Whole30-compliant meals ready to go, you are setting yourself up for success. It sounds simple, but the effectiveness of having a fridge stocked with wholesome, ready-to-eat foods cannot be overstated.

Moreover, by incorporating variety and ensuring that each meal is something you look forward to, the likelihood of sticking to your Whole30 commitment increases. The beauty of planning lies in its flexibility and ability to adjust to your busy week. If on certain days kitchen time is limited, knowing this ahead can shift your meal prep to less hectic days.

Therefore, mastering the art of planning in Whole30 is less about strict adherence to rules and more about creating a joy-filled journey with high-quality, nutritious foods that are both a pleasure to make and eat. As we dive deeper into this chapter, you'll gather the tools and strategies to not just cope, but excel, making each day of Whole30 an opportunity for health and discovery.

STRATEGIES FOR EFFECTIVE WHOLE30 DIET PLANNING

Imagine the Whole30 as a refreshing journey with a clear start and finish line. A successful journey requires not just a map, but strategic stops, well-paced steps, and foresight. Preparation is your guide, your compass on this transformative path, ensuring each step aligns with your health and wellness goals.

The essence of effective Whole30 diet planning revolves around understanding your personal, familial, and logistical circumstances. It's about matching your diet to your life's rhythm, ensuring that eating healthily doesn't become a chore, but a seamlessly integrated part of your daily routine. The strategies outlined here are designed to guide you through this process, blending practical advice with motivational insights.

Firstly, start with a deep dive into the Whole30 guidelines. Knowledge is power, and understanding what foods are Whole30 compliant and why certain foods are avoided will empower you to make informed choices. This isn't just about following a list, but about understanding the spirit of Whole30, which is to promote whole, unprocessed, and nourishing foods that revitalize and rejuvenate your body.

Transitioning from understanding to action, the initial step is to clear your kitchen of non-compliant items. This might seem drastic, but it's akin to setting up a clean workspace before starting a significant project – it minimizes distractions and temptations. Replace these items with Whole30 approved foods. Think of your kitchen as your fortress; what you bring inside will greatly influence your journey's outcome.

Next, the power of meal planning cannot be overstated. Each week, take a quiet moment to plan your meals. This doesn't need to be an elaborate activity; a simple chart or list of what you intend to eat for breakfast, lunch, and dinner can suffice. This planning phase is crucial as it not only saves time during the week but also reduces the mental load of deciding what to eat each day. Remember, each meal is a block building up to your success. When considering meal planning, also think about your schedule. Are there days filled with meetings? Does the school run leave you rushed? On busier days, plan simpler meals or consider prepping in advance. On quieter days, you might opt for recipes that are a bit more involved or allow for leftovers that can be integrated into the next day's meals. The aim here is to create a flexible, realistic meal schedule that ebbs and flows with your life's rhythm.

An effective strategy also involves batch cooking. Preparing large quantities of compliant meals that can be stored and eaten over several days can be a game-changer, especially on those days when time is not on your side. Consider roasting a variety of vegetables and grilling several pieces of chicken or fish that can be used in different ways throughout the week. This method not only saves time but also ensures that a healthy meal is always within reach.

Don't forget the psychological aspect of meal enjoyment. Variety is not just the spice of life but also the spice of Whole30. Rotate proteins, vegetables, and spices to keep your taste buds entertained and prevent monotony. Each meal should be something to look forward to, not a repetitive chore. Keep your meals colorful, diverse, and full of different textures to maintain excitement and satisfaction with your food choices.

Additionally, the inclusion of emergency snacks should be part of your plan. Whole30 compliant snack options like boiled eggs, nuts, or carrot sticks can be lifesavers when errands run long or when unexpected hunger strikes. Always having a healthy option at hand can mean the difference between staying on track or succumbing to temptations.

Furthermore, community support plays a pivotal role in sustained motivation. Whether it's family, friends, or online communities, sharing your journey can provide encouragement, swap meal ideas, and sustain motivation. Consider weekly check-ins with a friend who is also doing the Whole30 or joining online forums and groups. Here, experiences and tips are shared, and the feeling of a shared journey can make the path less daunting.

Lastly, keep a journal of your journey. Record not just what you eat but how you feel physically and emotionally. This record can be enlightening, showing you patterns or changes that may not be immediately obvious. It also serves as a reflection tool, helping you understand which foods work best for you and how your body responds to certain changes.

In conclusion, the success of the Whole30 diet hinges significantly on meticulous planning and preparation. By understanding the diet's foundations, setting up your environment for success, scheduling and prepping meals that align with your life, and leaning on community support, you equip yourself with the tools necessary to navigate this 30-day nutritional reset effectively. Remember, each day is a new opportunity to nourish your body, revitalize your health, and take proactive steps towards a lasting lifestyle of wellness. Through these efforts, Whole30 becomes less of a diet and more of a joyful, enriching journey towards better health and vitality.

CRAFTING A WEEKLY MEAL SCHEDULE

Embarking on the Whole30 journey is akin to mapping out a trip to an exciting, unexplored destination. Each meal is a stop along the way, providing fuel and nourishment enabling you to enjoy every part of the adventure. Crafting a weekly meal schedule is your itinerary; it organizes your journey, makes sure you have all you need before embarking, and ensures that you're not making unnecessary detours that pull you away from your destination of health and vitality.

Creating a successful meal schedule begins with a clear understanding of your weekly commitments. Much like how you would plan travel around flight schedules, considering your work meetings, children's activities, and personal commitments is key. Recognize the times when you'll need quick, easy meals and when you can afford the time to indulge in more elaborate culinary creations. This awareness allows you to sync your meal preparations effectively with your life's rhythms, ensuring that your diet supports rather than disrupts your daily activities.

Initiate this planning with a calm, relaxed planning session, ideally at a time when you feel refreshed and optimistic—perhaps a quiet Sunday morning. With your favorite drink in hand, lay out your week ahead on paper or a digital planner. Visualizing the week gives you a helicopter view, enabling you to spot potential high-stress days or the evenings when you might get home late. These insights are crucial for tailoring your meal prep to fit seamlessly into your life.

With your schedule in mind, the next step involves selecting recipes that align with your time availability and energy levels throughout the week. For instance, slow cooker recipes are perfect for long workdays. You can quickly set everything up in the morning and return home to a ready-to-eat meal. Conversely, days off might provide the perfect opportunity to try out new, more complex recipes that could also serve as fun, educational activities with your children or a partner.

To keep your meal plan exciting and sustainable, introduce a variety of proteins, fats, and carbohydrates. This rotation not only prevents dietary boredom but also ensures a wide range of nutrients are consumed, which is essential for your health. Imagine your plate as a palette of different colors with proteins, vegetables, healthy fats, and spices. The diversity in your meals stimulates your palate and ensures that eating healthy does not become a mundane task.

Moreover, consider the power of leftovers. Cook once, eat twice—or even thrice. Efficiently planned leftovers can serve as the basis for next-day lunches, saving you time and energy. A roasted chicken, for example, can be a savory dinner, a salad topping for lunch, and a hearty soup base for another dinner. This approach not only streamlines meal planning but also contributes to sustainable food practices, minimizing waste.

Inclusion of a few staple meals each week can also serve as an anchor in your meal schedule. These are meals you are familiar with and can prepare with ease. Not every meal has to be an elaborate affair; simplicity often breeds sustainability in a diet routine. These staple meals provide comfort and a reliable fallback when the unexpected occurs and time is limited.

This weekly meal planning also needs to incorporate snack planning. Having compliant snacks at hand can make the difference between steadfast adherence to your Whole30 journey and a hurried detour. Nuts, fruits, and pre-cut vegetables are excellent to have on hand, providing quick, nutritious options when hunger hits unexpectedly.

Collaborative family planning sessions can also add value to your meal scheduling. Gather input from your family members if you're cooking for more than just yourself. What are their favorite Whole30 compliant dishes? When do they feel they'll need more substantial meals during the week? This inclusivity not only eases your planning burden but also increases mealtime satisfaction across your household, making it easier for everyone to stay on track.

Another practical tip for your meal planning is to utilize digital tools and apps designed for meal planning. Many apps offer features like shopping lists, recipe organization, and even calorie trackers, which can simplify the process of staying within the Whole30 guidelines. Leveraging technology can make the task less daunting and more enjoyable.

Lastly, always leave room for flexibility in your meal plan. Life is unpredictable, and the ability to adjust while maintaining a focus on your health goals is vital. Maybe a work meeting runs late, or a family event is scheduled spontaneously—having quick backup options or being able to shuffle meals around ensures that your dietary goals aren't sidelined.

In sum, crafting a weekly meal schedule is less about strict adherence to a regimented plan and more about creating a flexible, enjoyable, and nourishing road map that guides you through your Whole30 journey. By strategically planning based on your personal and family calendar, embracing variety, planning for leftovers, and using technology, you set the stage for a successful, stress-free experience that not only meets your nutritional needs but also supports your dynamic lifestyle. This planned approach ensures that each meal is not just a fuel stop but a rewarding part of your greater journey towards health and vitality.

CHAPTER 3: BREAKFAST OPTIONS

Starting your day with a nourishing breakfast can truly transform the way you feel and function, making it a cornerstone of the Whole30 diet. In this chapter, we explore how beginning your morning with the right meal can set a positive tone for your entire day. Remember, breakfast isn't just another meal; it's your opportunity to fuel your body and empower yourself to tackle the challenges ahead with vigor and enthusiasm.

When I first embraced Whole30, I realized that my usual morning fare was doing little to provide me with the sustained energy I needed. The transition to a Whole30 breakfast was a revelation. No longer was I reaching for a mid-morning snack, ridden with hunger pangs; instead, I felt fuller longer, and my energy levels were more stable throughout the day.

Imagine sitting down to a plate filled with a vibrant mix of sautéed greens, topped with a perfectly poached egg and a side of savory sweet potato hash. Or perhaps a bowl of fresh fruit, sprinkled with seeds and nuts, accompanying a steaming mug of herbal tea sounds more to your liking. These are not just meals; they are messages to your body, affirming that you are cared for, nourished, and ready to rise to the day's demands.

In this chapter on breakfast options, we will delve into recipes that are both delightful to the palate and wonderfully simple to prepare. These dishes harness the natural goodness of whole foods, each ingredient chosen not just for its flavor, but for its contribution to your health. We'll discover how spices can not only elevate the taste but also boost your metabolism, how the right fats can enhance mental clarity, and how the simplicity of a well-prepared dish can bring joy to your morning routine.

Transitioning to a whole food-focused breakfast might seem daunting at first, especially if your mornings are typically rushed. However, the recipes provided here are designed to fit into even the busiest of schedules, ensuring that you can enjoy a wholesome, delicious start to your day without stress. This is not just about eating; it's about transforming your morning ritual into a nurturing practice that sets you up for success. Let's make every breakfast a stepping stone to a healthier, happier you.

SUNRISE SWEET POTATO AND KALE HASH

Preparation Time: 15 min
Cooking Time: 20 min
Mode of Cooking: Sautéing
Servings: 4 Serv.
Ingredients:

- 2 medium sweet potatoes, peeled and diced
- 1 bunch kale, stems removed and leaves chopped
- 1 large onion, diced
- 4 cloves garlic, minced
- 1 red bell pepper, diced
- 2 Tbsp olive oil
- 4 large eggs
- Sea salt to taste
- Freshly ground black pepper to taste

Directions:

1. Heat olive oil in a large skillet over medium heat
2. Add diced sweet potatoes and sauté until slightly tender, about 7 min
3. Add onion, bell pepper, and garlic and continue to sauté until onion is translucent

4. Stir in chopped kale and cook until wilted

5. Create four wells in the hash and crack an egg into each well

6. Cover skillet and cook until eggs are set, about 5 min

7. Season with salt and pepper

Tips:

- Serve with a dash of hot sauce for added kick

- Opt for kale with smaller leaves for more tenderness

- For a vegan option, substitute eggs with tofu scramble

Nutritional Values: Calories: 310, Fat: 15g, Carbs: 35g, Protein: 13g, Sugar: 6g, Sodium: 320 mg, Potassium: 670 mg, Cholesterol: 186 mg

COCONUT-CASHEW BREAKFAST SKILLET

Preparation Time: 10 min
Cooking Time: 15 min
Mode of Cooking: Sautéing
Servings: 2
Ingredients:

- 1 cup cashew nuts, unsalted

- 1 large sweet plantain, peeled and sliced

- 1 Tbsp coconut oil

- ½ tsp ground cinnamon

- Pinch of sea salt

- 1 cup coconut flakes, unsweetened

- ¼ cup golden raisins

- 2 tsp freshly grated ginger

Directions:

1. Heat coconut oil in a skillet over medium heat

2. Add sliced plantain and sauté until golden and caramelized, about 8 min

3. Stir in cashews, coconut flakes, ground cinnamon, and sea salt and cook until cashews are lightly toasted

4. Finish with freshly grated ginger and golden raisins, stirring well to combine

Tips:

- Experiment with using banana instead of plantain for a different sweetness profile

- Ensure not to burn the coconut flakes by constantly stirring the mixture

Nutritional Values: Calories: 505, Fat: 32g, Carbs: 53g, Protein: 10g, Sugar: 20g, Sodium: 100 mg, Potassium: 540 mg, Cholesterol: 0 mg

AVOCADO AND TOMATO OMELET

Preparation Time: 10 min
Cooking Time: 10 min
Mode of Cooking: Frying
Servings: 2
Ingredients:

- 4 large eggs

- 1 ripe avocado, peeled and sliced
- 1 medium tomato, chopped
- 1 Tbsp ghee
- Sea salt to taste
- Freshly ground black pepper to taste
- 1 Tbsp fresh cilantro, chopped

Directions:

1. Beat eggs in a bowl and season with salt and pepper
2. Heat ghee in a non-stick skillet over medium heat
3. Pour in the eggs and cook until they begin to set around the edges
4. Layer sliced avocado and chopped tomatoes on one half of the omelet and fold over to encase the filling
5. Continue cooking until eggs are fully set
6. Garnish with fresh cilantro

Tips:

- Add some crushed red pepper if you enjoy a bit of heat
- Using ripe, creamy avocados will enhance the texture of your omelet

Nutritional Values: Calories: 390, Fat: 31g, Carbs: 12g, Protein: 18g, Sugar: 4g, Sodium: 420 mg, Potassium: 830 mg, Cholesterol: 372 mg

---

SPICED PUMPKIN AND ALMOND BUTTER SMOOTHIE

Preparation Time: 5 min
Cooking Time: none
Mode of Cooking: Blending
Servings: 2
Ingredients:

- ½ cup pumpkin puree
- 1 banana, frozen
- 2 Tbsp almond butter, unsweetened
- 1 cup almond milk, unsweetened
- ½ tsp ground cinnamon
- ¼ tsp ground nutmeg
- 1 Tbsp chia seeds
- Ice cubes as needed

Directions:

1. Combine pumpkin puree, frozen banana, almond butter, almond milk, cinnamon, nutmeg, and chia seeds in a blender
2. Blend until smooth
3. Add ice cubes and blend again until desired consistency is achieved

Tips:

- Try adding a scoop of Whole30-compliant vanilla protein powder for an extra protein boost
- If the smoothie is too thick, adjust by adding more almond milk

Nutritional Values: Calories: 265, Fat: 15g, Carbs: 30g, Protein: 6g, Sugar: 12g, Sodium: 95 mg, Potassium: 410 mg, Cholesterol: 0 mg

SAVORY MUSHROOM AND HERB FRITTATA

Preparation Time: 10 min
Cooking Time: 25 min
Mode of Cooking: Baking
Servings: 4
Ingredients:

- 8 large eggs
- 1 cup mushrooms, sliced
- 1 small onion, diced
- 2 Tbsp fresh parsley, chopped
- 1 Tbsp fresh thyme leaves
- 2 Tbsp ghee
- Sea salt to taste
- Freshly ground black pepper to taste

Directions:

1. Preheat oven to 375°F (190°C)
2. In a mixing bowl, whisk eggs with salt and pepper
3. Heat ghee in an oven-safe skillet over medium heat
4. Sauté onion until translucent
5. Add mushrooms and herbs and cook until mushrooms are soft
6. Pour the eggs over the sautéed mushrooms and herbs
7. Transfer skillet to oven and bake until the frittata is set and golden on top, about 15 min

Tips:

- Serve with a side of mixed greens for a complete breakfast
- Fresh herbs can be substituted with dried herbs if fresh are not available
- A sprinkle of nutritional yeast will add a cheesy flavor without dairy

Nutritional Values: Calories: 240, Fat: 18g, Carbs: 7g, Protein: 15g, Sugar: 3g, Sodium: 210 mg, Potassium: 230 mg, Cholesterol: 372 mg

COCONUT CINNAMON CELERIAC MUFFINS

Preparation Time: 10 min
Cooking Time: 25 min
Mode of Cooking: Baking
Servings: 6
Ingredients:

- 2 cups grated celeriac
- ½ cup unsweetened shredded coconut
- ¼ cup coconut flour
- ½ tsp baking soda
- 1 tsp cinnamon

- ¼ tsp salt
- 4 eggs, beaten
- ½ cup apple sauce
- ¼ cup coconut oil, melted
- 1 tsp vanilla extract

Directions:

1. Preheat oven to 350°F (175°C)
2. Mix coconut flour, shredded coconut, baking soda, cinnamon, and salt in a bowl
3. In another bowl, combine eggs, apple sauce, melted coconut oil, and vanilla extract
4. Combine wet and dry ingredients, stir in grated celeriac
5. Spoon batter into muffin tins and bake for 25 min

Tips:

- Muffins can be stored in an airtight container for up to 4 days or frozen for longer storage
- Serve with a smear of almond butter for extra richness

Nutritional Values: Calories: 214, Fat: 15g, Carbs: 16g, Protein: 6g, Sugar: 4g, Sodium: 320 mg, Potassium: 90 mg, Cholesterol: 121 mg

AVOCADO LIME SHRIMP SALAD

Preparation Time: 10 min
Cooking Time: none
Mode of Cooking: Tossing
Servings: 2
Ingredients:

- 1 large ripe avocado, diced
- 1 cup cooked shrimp, tails removed
- 1 cup cherry tomatoes, halved
- ½ cucumber, diced
- ¼ red onion, thinly sliced
- 2 Tbsp olive oil
- Juice of 1 lime
- Salt and black pepper to taste
- ¼ cup fresh cilantro, chopped

Directions:

1. Combine diced avocado, shrimp, cherry tomatoes, and cucumber in a bowl
2. Add red onion, olive oil, lime juice, salt, and black pepper, and gently toss to combine
3. Garnish with chopped cilantro

Tips:

- Serve immediately for best texture, or chill to let flavors meld
- Boost nutrients by adding a handful of baby spinach or arugula

Nutritional Values: Calories: 297, Fat: 21g, Carbs: 12g, Protein: 17g, Sugar: 2g, Sodium: 112 mg, Potassium: 564 mg, Cholesterol: 120 mg

SMOKED SALMON AND ASPARAGUS FRITTATA

Preparation Time: 10 min
Cooking Time: 15 min
Mode of Cooking: Baking
Servings: 4
Ingredients:

- 6 eggs
- ¼ cup coconut milk
- 1 tsp dill, chopped
- Salt and black pepper to taste
- 1 Tbsp olive oil
- 1 cup asparagus, chopped
- 4 oz smoked salmon, chopped
- ¼ cup red bell pepper, diced

Directions:

1. Preheat oven to 400°F (204°C)
2. Whisk eggs, coconut milk, dill, salt, and pepper in a bowl
3. Heat olive oil in an oven-safe skillet over medium heat
4. Sauté asparagus and bell pepper until tender, about 5 min
5. Reduce heat, add egg mixture and smoked salmon, cook until edges set, about 5 min
6. Transfer skillet to oven, bake until frittata is fully set, about 10 min

Tips:

- Ideal for meal prep, can be refrigerated and reheated
- Serve with a side of mixed greens tossed with lemon vinaigrette

Nutritional Values: Calories: 235, Fat: 15g, Carbs: 4g, Protein: 20g, Sugar: 2g, Sodium: 540 mg, Potassium: 340 mg, Cholesterol: 275 mg

PALEO PLANTAIN PANCAKES

Preparation Time: 10 min
Cooking Time: 15 min
Mode of Cooking: Pan-frying
Servings: 3
Ingredients:

- 2 large ripe plantains, peeled and mashed
- 3 eggs
- 1 tsp vanilla extract
- ½ tsp baking powder
- 1 Tbsp coconut oil, for cooking
- Maple syrup, for serving (optional)

Directions:

1. Combine mashed plantains, eggs, vanilla extract, and baking powder in a bowl until smooth
2. Heat coconut oil in a skillet over medium heat

3. Pour ¼ cup of batter for each pancake, cook until bubbles form on the surface, about 3 min
4. Flip and cook until golden, about 2 min

Tips:

- Serve hot with a drizzle of maple syrup, if desired
- Pancakes can be topped with fresh berries or banana slices for added sweetness

Nutritional Values: Calories: 241, Fat: 8g, Carbs: 38g, Protein: 6g, Sugar: 16g, Sodium: 200 mg, Potassium: 750 mg, Cholesterol: 185 mg

---

GREEN PLANTAIN BREAKFAST HASH

Preparation Time: 15 min
Cooking Time: 20 min
Mode of Cooking: Stovetop
Servings: 2
Ingredients:

- 1 large green plantain, peeled and diced
- 1 small red onion, chopped
- 1 bell pepper, diced
- 2 cloves garlic, minced
- 2 Tbsp coconut oil
- 4 oz diced cooked ham
- Salt and pepper to taste

Directions:

1. Heat coconut oil in a skillet over medium heat
2. Add plantains and sauté until golden, about 5 min
3. Add onion, bell pepper, and garlic, cook until softened
4. Stir in cooked ham, season with salt and pepper, and cook until everything is heated through

Tips:

- Try using green plantains for a firmer texture
- Can substitute ham with other Whole30 compliant proteins like diced chicken or pork

Nutritional Values: Calories: 330, Fat: 14g, Carbs: 45g, Protein: 10g, Sugar: 21g, Sodium: 70 mg, Potassium: 650 mg, Cholesterol: 30 mg

---

SUNRISE CITRUS SALAD

Preparation Time: 10 min
Cooking Time: none
Mode of Cooking: No Cooking
Servings: 4
Ingredients:

- 2 ruby red grapefruits, peeled and sectioned
- 2 oranges, peeled and sectioned
- 1 tsp fresh mint, chopped
- 1 Tbsp lime juice
- 1 Tbsp olive oil

- Salt and black pepper to taste

Directions:

1. Combine grapefruit and orange sections in a bowl
2. Mix lime juice, olive oil, mint, salt, and pepper in a small jar and shake well
3. Pour dressing over citrus sections and toss gently

Tips:

- This salad can be served with a sprinkle of chia seeds for added nutrients
- Refrigerate for at least one hour before serving to blend flavors

Nutritional Values: Calories: 105, Fat: 2.5g, Carbs: 22g, Protein: 2g, Sugar: 15g, Sodium: 5 mg, Potassium: 300 mg, Cholesterol: 0 mg

SAVORY BREAKFAST MUFFINS

Preparation Time: 15 min
Cooking Time: 25 min
Mode of Cooking: Baking
Servings: 6
Ingredients:

- 3 cups almond flour
- 1 Tbsp coconut flour
- 6 large eggs
- 1/2 cup unsweetened almond milk
- 1 Tbsp olive oil
- 1 tsp baking powder
- 1/2 tsp salt
- 1 cup fresh spinach, chopped
- 1/2 cup sun-dried tomatoes, chopped
- 1/4 cup fresh basil, chopped

Directions:

1. Preheat oven to 350°F (175°C)
2. Combine almond flour, coconut flour, baking powder, and salt in a bowl
3. In another bowl, whisk eggs, almond milk, and oil
4. Mix dry and wet ingredients, fold in spinach, sun-dried tomatoes, and basil
5. Spoon into muffin tins and bake for 25 min

Tips:

- Experiment by adding different herbs like oregano or parsley for variety
- These muffins can be stored in the refrigerator for up to a week

Nutritional Values: Calories: 270, Fat: 22g, Carbs: 8g, Protein: 13g, Sugar: 2g, Sodium: 300 mg, Potassium: 200 mg, Cholesterol: 185 mg

CHAPTER 4: TASTY AND NUTRITIOUS SALADS

Welcome to the world of salads — a fresh, vibrant universe of colors, textures, and flavors that promise to delight your palate while fueling your body with everything good. It's easy to underestimate the humble salad, often pigeonholed as just a simple side. But let's transcend typical expectations together and explore how these dishes can stand proudly as centerpieces of a wholesome, Whole30-compliant meal.

Imagine you're walking through a bustling farmers' market. Each stall bursts with the season's freshest produce; crisp lettuces, radiant peppers, juicy tomatoes, and herbs so aromatic you can almost taste their flavors with your nose. This chapter is your guide to transforming these natural treasures into salads that resonate with vibrancy and satisfaction.

Building a nourishing salad is an art that balances variety in texture with harmony in flavor. It's about creating a meal that satisfies without weighing you down, perfectly aligning with the Whole30 ethos of health and vitality. Each recipe here is crafted to introduce you to unexpected combinations — sweet, crunchy apples nestled among bitter greens, or spicy arugula softened by creamy avocado.

Moreover, these salads aren't just about sticking to your Whole30 commitment; they're about reveling in the possibilities that each day of the program offers. They're quick to prepare, ideal for those bustling days when time is scarce but you're committed to eating well. With these recipes, a nourishing meal that fits into your Whole30 journey is only a few minutes away.

This chapter ensures that salads are never bland or repetitive but are instead a daily adventure in taste and health. It's designed to make you feel good about what you're eating and confident in your ability to maintain a wholesome diet that doesn't skimp on flavor or satisfaction.

So, grab your salad bowl and let's dive into a world where meals are as nutritious as they are delightful. Each bite is a step forward in your journey to health, energizing your body and uplifting your spirit.

SMOKED SALMON AND AVOCADO CITRUS SALAD

Preparation Time: 20 min.
Cooking Time: none
Mode of Cooking: No Cooking
Servings: 4
Ingredients:

- 4 cups arugula
- 200g smoked salmon, sliced
- 2 avocados, sliced
- 1 ruby grapefruit, segments
- 1 bulb fennel, thinly sliced
- Dressing: 2 Tbsp extra virgin olive oil
- 1 Tbsp apple cider vinegar
- 1 tsp fresh lemon juice
- 1 tsp Dijon mustard
- Salt and pepper to taste

Directions:

1. Combine arugula, fennel, avocado, grapefruit segments, and smoked salmon in a large salad bowl
2. In a separate bowl, whisk together extra virgin olive oil, apple cider vinegar, lemon juice, and Dijon mustard until emulsified
3. Drizzle the dressing over the salad and gently toss to coat

Tips:
- Use a mandoline for thinly slicing the fennel for a more delicate texture in the salad
- Incorporate additional herbs like dill or parsley to enhance flavor

Nutritional Values: Calories: 240, Fat: 15g, Carbs: 12g, Protein: 15g, Sugar: 5g, Sodium: 470 mg, Potassium: 650 mg, Cholesterol: 30 mg

WARM SPICED BEETROOT SALAD WITH PECANS

Preparation Time: 15 min.
Cooking Time: 30 min.
Mode of Cooking: Roasting
Servings: 4
Ingredients:
- 4 medium beetroots, peeled and diced
- 1 red onion, thinly sliced
- 2 Tbsp coconut oil, melted
- 1 tsp ground cumin
- ½ tsp smoked paprika
- Salt and pepper to taste
- 1 cup pecans, toasted
- For the dressing: 2 Tbsp balsamic vinegar
- 1 Tbsp olive oil
- 1 garlic clove, minced
- 1 tsp Whole30 compliant mustard

Directions:
1. Preheat oven to 375°F (190°C)
2. Toss diced beetroots and red onion with coconut oil, cumin, paprika, salt, and pepper
3. Roast in the preheated oven for 30 minutes, stirring halfway through
4. Allow to cool slightly before adding toasted pecans
5. Mix balsamic vinegar, olive oil, garlic, and mustard for dressing and pour over the salad

Tips:
- Toast pecans in a dry skillet for an enhanced nutty flavor
- Serve salad warm for a comforting feel

Nutritional Values: Calories: 295, Fat: 24g, Carbs: 18g, Protein: 4g, Sugar: 12g, Sodium: 180 mg, Potassium: 400 mg, Cholesterol: 0 mg

THYME-ROASTED CARROT RIBBON SALAD WITH ALMONDS

Preparation Time: 20 min.
Cooking Time: 25 min.
Mode of Cooking: Roasting
Servings: 4
Ingredients:
- 6 large carrots, peeled into ribbons
- 3 Tbsp olive oil

- 1 Tbsp fresh thyme leaves
- Salt and pepper to taste
- ¼ cup slivered almonds, toasted
- 2 Tbsp lemon juice

Directions:

1. Preheat oven to 400°F (205°C)
2. Toss carrot ribbons in olive oil, fresh thyme, salt, and pepper
3. Spread on a baking sheet and roast for 25 min., turning occasionally until crisp and tender
4. Combine warm carrots with lemon juice and slivered almonds before serving

Tips:

- Carrot ribbons can be prepared using a vegetable peeler for an elegant presentation
- Almonds add a satisfying crunch and boost of protein

Nutritional Values: Calories: 210, Fat: 15g, Carbs: 18g, Protein: 3g, Sugar: 8g, Sodium: 110 mg, Potassium: 520 mg, Cholesterol: 0 mg

---

CRISPY KALE AND APPLE SALAD WITH WALNUT VINAIGRETTE

Preparation Time: 15 min.
Cooking Time: 10 min.
Mode of Cooking: Blanching and Cooling
Servings: 4
Ingredients:

- 4 cups kale, stems removed and leaves torn
- 1 apple, thinly sliced
- ½ cup walnuts, toasted
- 3 Tbsp walnut oil
- 1 Tbsp cider vinegar
- 1 tsp honey (omit for Whole30 compliance, or use a date paste)
- Salt and pepper to taste

Directions:

1. Blanch kale in boiling water for 2 min., then rinse under cold water and dry thoroughly
2. Combine walnut oil, cider vinegar, and honey/date paste in a bowl and whisk to form vinaigrette
3. Toss kale, apple slices, and walnuts in the dressing

Tips:

- Massage kale leaves briefly after blanching to make them softer and easier to digest
- The natural sweetness of apples contrasts delightfully with the savory notes of the dressing

Nutritional Values: Calories: 255, Fat: 21g, Carbs: 16g, Protein: 5g, Sugar: 10g (omit if using date paste), Sodium: 125 mg, Potassium: 390 mg, Cholesterol: 0 mg

---

SPICY SHRIMP AND CUCUMBER SALAD

Preparation Time: 10 min.
Cooking Time: 5 min.
Mode of Cooking: Sautéing
Servings: 4

Ingredients:

- 200g shrimp, peeled and deveined
- 1 large cucumber, spiralized or thinly sliced
- 1 red bell pepper, thinly sliced
- 2 Tbsp olive oil
- 1 tsp chili flakes
- 1 tsp paprika
- Salt to taste
- For dressing: 2 Tbsp lime juice
- 1 Tbsp fish sauce
- 1 Tbsp chopped cilantro
- 1 small garlic clove, minced

Directions:

1. Heat olive oil in a skillet over medium heat
2. Add shrimp, chili flakes, paprika, and salt, sautéing until shrimp are pink and cooked through, about 5 min.
3. Mix lime juice, fish sauce, cilantro, and garlic to create dressing
4. Toss cooked shrimp with cucumber, bell pepper, and dressing

Tips:

- For a crunchier texture, chill the salad before serving
- Adding avocado slices can provide creaminess and satisfying richness to this light salad

Nutritional Values: Calories: 180, Fat: 11g, Carbs: 8g, Protein: 14g, Sugar: 3g, Sodium: 670 mg, Potassium: 320 mg, Cholesterol: 115 mg

SPICED KALE AND APPLE SALAD

Preparation Time: 15 min.
Cooking Time: none
Mode of Cooking: No Cooking
Servings: 4
Ingredients:

- 2 bunches kale, stems removed and leaves finely chopped
- 1 crisp apple, such as Honeycrisp or Fuji, thinly sliced
- 1/4 cup toasted almonds, sliced
- 1/4 cup dried cranberries
- 1/2 red onion, thinly sliced
- For Dressing: 3 Tbsp extra virgin olive oil
- 2 Tbsp apple cider vinegar
- 1 tsp Dijon mustard
- 1 tsp raw honey (omit for strict Whole30)
- Salt and pepper to taste

Directions:

1. Combine kale, apple slices, toasted almonds, dried cranberries, and red onion in a large salad bowl

2. In a small bowl, whisk together olive oil, apple cider vinegar, Dijon mustard, raw honey if using, salt, and pepper
3. Pour dressing over salad mixture and toss to coat thoroughly

Tips:
- Massage the kale leaves with a bit of olive oil before adding other ingredients to soften the texture
- Add grilled chicken or shrimp to make this salad a hearty meal
- If strictly following Whole30, omit honey and sweeten the dressing lightly with fresh orange juice

Nutritional Values: Calories: 210, Fat: 14g, Carbs: 20g, Protein: 4g, Sugar: 10g (omit honey for less), Sodium: 65 mg, Potassium: 449 mg, Cholesterol: 0 mg

ROASTED BEET AND CITRUS SALAD

Preparation Time: 10 min.
Cooking Time: 45 min.
Mode of Cooking: Roasting
Servings: 4
Ingredients:
- 4 medium beets, scrubbed and cut into wedges
- 2 oranges, peeled and segments separated
- 1/2 cup walnut halves, toasted
- 1/4 cup thinly sliced fennel
- For Dressing: 3 Tbsp avocado oil
- 1 Tbsp balsamic vinegar
- Salt and pepper to taste

Directions:
1. Roast beet wedges in a preheated oven at 400°F (204°C) until tender and caramelized, about 45 min.
2. Allow beets to cool slightly, then mix with orange segments, walnut halves, and sliced fennel in a salad bowl
3. Whisk together avocado oil, balsamic vinegar, salt, and pepper to make dressing
4. Drizzle dressing over salad just before serving

Tips:
- Serve this salad with a sprinkle of fresh mint or parsley to enhance flavor and freshness
- Beet skins can be left on for additional nutritional benefits, including fiber and vitamins
- Refrigerate leftovers promptly to preserve freshness and prevent sogginess

Nutritional Values: Calories: 252, Fat: 18g, Carbs: 22g, Protein: 6g, Sugar: 16g, Sodium: 86 mg, Potassium: 547 mg, Cholesterol: 0 mg

AVOCADO AND SHRIMP CEVICHE SALAD

Preparation Time: 15 min.
Cooking Time: none
Mode of Cooking: Marination
Servings: 4
Ingredients:
- 1 lb fresh shrimp, peeled, deveined and chopped

- 2 ripe avocados, diced
- 1/2 cup cucumber, diced
- 1/4 cup red onion, minced
- 1/4 cup cilantro, chopped
- Juice of 2 limes
- 1 tsp extra virgin olive oil
- Salt and pepper to taste

Directions:

1. Combine shrimp, lime juice, and olive oil in a mixing bowl, and let marinate for 10 min.
2. Add diced avocados, cucumber, red onion, and cilantro to the marinated shrimp
3. Mix gently to combine, seasoning with salt and pepper to taste

Tips:

- This salad is best served immediately to enjoy its freshness
- Add a dash of chili powder or sliced jalapeño for an extra kick
- Pair with coconut water or a crisp, dry white wine for a delightful meal

Nutritional Values: Calories: 290, Fat: 17g, Carbs: 12g, Protein: 25g, Sugar: 2g, Sodium: 345 mg, Potassium: 640 mg, Cholesterol: 180 mg

MEDITERRANEAN TOMATO AND CUCUMBER SALAD

Preparation Time: 10 min.
Cooking Time: none
Mode of Cooking: No Cooking
Servings: 4
Ingredients:

- 3 medium tomatoes, chopped
- 1 large cucumber, diced
- 1/4 cup red onion, thinly sliced
- 1/4 cup Kalamata olives, pitted and halved
- 1/4 cup fresh basil, chopped
- For Dressing: 3 Tbsp extra virgin olive oil
- 1 Tbsp red wine vinegar
- 1 garlic clove, minced
- Salt and pepper to taste

Directions:

1. Combine tomatoes, cucumber, red onion, Kalamata olives, and fresh basil in a large salad bowl
2. In a small bowl, whisk together extra virgin olive oil, red wine vinegar, minced garlic, salt, and pepper
3. Pour dressing over salad mixture just before serving and toss gently to coat

Tips:

- Garnish with feta cheese crumbles for an added layer of flavor, if not strictly following Whole30
- This salad pairs wonderfully with grilled fish or rotisserie chicken for a complete meal

Nutritional Values: Calories: 140, Fat: 12g, Carbs: 9g, Protein: 2g, Sugar: 5g, Sodium: 150 mg, Potassium: 372 mg, Cholesterol: 0 mg

SPICY THAI MANGO SALAD WITH CASHEWS

Preparation Time: 20 min.
Cooking Time: none
Mode of Cooking: No Cooking
Servings: 4
Ingredients:

- 2 ripe mangoes, julienned
- 1/2 cup cashews, toasted and roughly chopped
- 1/2 red bell pepper, thinly sliced
- 1/4 cup fresh cilantro, chopped
- 1/4 cup fresh mint, chopped
- 1 small red chili, deseeded and finely chopped
- For Dressing: Juice of 1 lime
- 2 Tbsp fish sauce (omit for strict Whole30)
- 1 Tbsp coconut aminos
- 1 tsp raw honey (omit for strict Whole30)
- 1 garlic clove, minced

Directions:

1. Combine julienned mangoes, toasted cashews, red bell pepper, cilantro, mint, and red chili in a large salad bowl
2. In a small bowl, whisk together lime juice, fish sauce if using, coconut aminos, raw honey if using, and minced garlic
3. Pour dressing over salad mixture and toss well to combine

Tips:

- To make this salad Whole30 compliant, omit fish sauce and honey
- Serve immediately after dressing to maintain crunch from the vegetables
- Pair with grilled seafood or poultry for a refreshing and light meal

Nutritional Values: Calories: 214, Fat: 8g, Carbs: 35g, Protein: 3g, Sugar: 29g (omit honey for less), Sodium: 320 mg, Potassium: 495 mg, Cholesterol: 0 mg

SPICED CARROT AND AVOCADO SALAD

Preparation Time: 15 min.
Cooking Time: none
Mode of Cooking: No Cooking
Servings: 4
Ingredients:

- 3 cups shredded carrots
- 2 ripe avocados, diced
- 1/4 cup crushed walnuts
- 1 small red onion, thinly sliced
- 2 Tbsp fresh cilantro, chopped
- 2 Tbsp olive oil
- 1 Tbsp fresh lemon juice

- 1 tsp cumin
- 1/2 tsp paprika
- Salt and pepper to taste

Directions:

1. Combine shredded carrots, diced avocados, crushed walnuts, and sliced red onion in a large bowl
2. In a separate bowl, whisk together olive oil, lemon juice, cumin, paprika, salt, and pepper to create the dressing
3. Pour dressing over the salad and gently toss to combine
4. Garnish with fresh cilantro before serving

Tips:

- Serve immediately to prevent avocados from browning
- Add grilled chicken or shrimp for extra protein
- If not serving immediately, add avocado just before serving to maintain freshness

Nutritional Values: Calories: 220, Fat: 17g, Carbs: 18g, Protein: 4g, Sugar: 7g, Sodium: 70mg, Potassium: 690mg, Cholesterol: 0mg

KALE AND BRUSSEL SPROUT SLAW

Preparation Time: 20 min.
Cooking Time: none
Mode of Cooking: No Cooking
Servings: 4
Ingredients:

- 3 cups chopped kale
- 2 cups shredded Brussels sprouts
- 1/4 cup almonds, slivered
- 1/3 cup dried cranberries
- 2 Tbsp ghee, melted
- 1 Tbsp apple cider vinegar
- 1 tsp Dijon mustard
- 1 Tbsp lemon juice
- Salt and pepper to taste

Directions:

1. Combine chopped kale and shredded Brussels sprouts in a large bowl
2. In a smaller bowl, mix together melted ghee, apple cider vinegar, Dijon mustard, lemon juice, salt, and pepper to make the dressing
3. Pour the dressing over the kale and Brussels sprouts, tossing thoroughly to coat
4. Add slivered almonds and dried cranberries, tossing again to distribute evenly

Tips:

- Massage the kale with your hands before adding other ingredients to soften its texture
- This salad maintains its texture well, making it perfect for prepare-ahead meals

Nutritional Values: Calories: 160, Fat: 9g, Carbs: 18g, Protein: 4g, Sugar: 9g, Sodium: 115mg, Potassium: 350mg, Cholesterol: 15mg

CHAPTER 5: HEARTY SOUPS AND STEWS RICH IN NUTRIENTS

There's something profoundly comforting about stirring a steaming pot of soup or stew, watching as the simple ingredients meld into a harmonious and nourishing meal. In Chapter 5, we explore the world of hearty soups and stews, each recipe brimming with nutrients that promise not just to fill your stomach, but to replenish your health and energize your body.

Imagine coming home on a brisk day to a pot of rich beef stew simmering gently, its aroma filling your kitchen, or waking up on a Sunday morning to a vibrant, vegetable-packed minestrone that's been marrying flavors overnight in your slow cooker. These are the moments that highlight the sheer joy and simplicity of using whole foods to support our well-being.

Soups and stews are particularly magical for their ability to transform basic ingredients into deeply flavorful dishes that can be both healing and invigorating. They allow us to get creative with seasonal produce and lean proteins, incorporating spices and herbs that not only boost flavor but also offer impressive health benefits. Turmeric, ginger, garlic, and fresh leafy greens turn a simple broth into a powerhouse of anti-inflammatory and immune-enhancing properties.

What stands out about this chapter is not just the recipes themselves, but the method behind them—how a slow simmer can deepen flavors, how a splash of freshness added at the end can lift a dish, and how flexible these recipes can be. Adaptability is key; whether you're a busy parent trying to feed a family or someone looking to prepare single-serving meals that last all week, soups and stews can be tailored to suit any dietary need and schedule.

This chapter, rich with nutrients and variety, ensures that your Whole30 journey is not just about what you can't eat, but celebrates what you can. Each recipe is designed to be straightforward with a focus on ingredients that build a foundation for a healthier lifestyle, proving that wholesome eating doesn't have to come at the expense of flavor or satisfaction. Gear up to stir, simmer, and nourish your way to better health with easy-to-follow, delicious recipes that make staying on track a delightful experience.

SAFFRON INFUSED SUNSHINE STEW

Preparation Time: 15 min
Cooking Time: 45 min
Mode of Cooking: Stovetop
Servings: 4
Ingredients:

- 2 Tbsp olive oil
- 1 lb chicken thighs, boneless and skinless, cut into pieces
- 1 large onion, chopped
- 3 cloves garlic, minced
- 1 tsp turmeric
- 1 pinch saffron threads
- 1 qt chicken stock
- 2 large carrots, sliced
- 1 sweet potato, peeled and cubed
- 1 red bell pepper, diced
- 1 zucchini, sliced
- Salt and pepper to taste

Directions:

1. Heat olive oil in a large pot over medium heat
2. Add chicken pieces and sauté until browned
3. Add onions and garlic, cook until soft
4. Stir in turmeric and saffron, cook for 1 min
5. Pour in chicken stock and bring to a simmer
6. Add carrots, sweet potato, bell pepper, and zucchini
7. Simmer for 30 min or until vegetables are tender
8. Season with salt and pepper

Tips:

- Add a squeeze of fresh lemon juice for extra zest
- Serve with a side of steamed green beans for a balanced meal

Nutritional Values: Calories: 350, Fat: 18g, Carbs: 24g, Protein: 28g, Sugar: 8g, Sodium: 750mg, Potassium: 900mg, Cholesterol: 100mg

HERBED COCONUT AND SHRIMP BROTH

Preparation Time: 20 min
Cooking Time: 30 min
Mode of Cooking: Stovetop
Servings: 4
Ingredients:

- 1 Tbsp coconut oil
- 1 lb shrimp, peeled and deveined
- 1 onion, finely chopped
- 2 cloves garlic, minced
- 1 tsp ginger, minced
- 2 Tbsp fresh cilantro, chopped
- 1 Tbsp fresh basil, chopped
- 1 can (14 oz.) coconut milk
- 2 cups vegetable broth
- 1 lime, juiced
- Salt and pepper to taste

Directions:

1. Heat coconut oil in a saucepan over medium heat
2. Sauté onion, garlic, and ginger until onion is translucent
3. Add shrimp and cook until they turn pink
4. Pour in coconut milk and vegetable broth, bring to a low boil
5. Add cilantro and basil, simmer for 10 min
6. Stir in lime juice and season with salt and pepper

Tips:

- Enhance the flavor by adding a dash of fish sauce
- Garnish with additional basil leaves before serving

- Perfect paired with cauliflower rice for a complete meal

Nutritional Values: Calories: 280, Fat: 22g, Carbs: 8g, Protein: 16g, Sugar: 2g, Sodium: 480mg, Potassium: 350mg, Cholesterol: 115mg

RUSTIC BEEF AND ROOT VEGETABLE STEW

Preparation Time: 20 min
Cooking Time: 2 hr
Mode of Cooking: Slow Cooker
Servings: 6
Ingredients:

- 1 lb beef chuck, cut into cubes
- 1 Tbsp olive oil
- 2 parsnips, peeled and chopped
- 2 turnips, peeled and chopped
- 1 onion, chopped
- 3 cloves garlic, minced
- 2 qt beef broth
- 1 Tbsp fresh rosemary, chopped
- 1 tsp black pepper
- Salt to taste

Directions:

1. Brown beef cubes in olive oil in a skillet over medium-high heat and transfer to slow cooker
2. Add parsnips, turnips, onion, and garlic to the slow cooker
3. Pour beef broth over the ingredients, ensuring they are covered
4. Stir in rosemary and pepper
5. Cook on low for 8 hrs or until beef is tender and vegetables are cooked
6. Season with salt

Tips:

- Thicken the stew by mashing some of the vegetables
- Serve hot, topped with a sprinkle of fresh parsley for added color and flavor
- Ideal with a slice of homemade almond flour bread

Nutritional Values: Calories: 330, Fat: 20g, Carbs: 15g, Protein: 25g, Sugar: 5g, Sodium: 690mg, Potassium: 800mg, Cholesterol: 80mg

LEMON-HERB CHICKEN AND SPINACH SOUP

Preparation Time: 10 min
Cooking Time: 25 min
Mode of Cooking: Stovetop
Servings: 4
Ingredients:

- 2 Tbsp ghee
- 1 lb chicken breast, diced
- 1 onion, diced

- 3 cups spinach, fresh
- 1 lemon, zest and juice
- 4 cups chicken broth
- 1 tsp dried oregano
- Salt and pepper to taste

Directions:

1. Heat ghee in a large pot over medium heat
2. Add diced chicken and cook until no longer pink
3. Add onion and sauté until translucent
4. Stir in lemon zest and juice, then pour in chicken broth
5. Bring to a boil, then reduce to simmer
6. Add spinach and oregano, cook for 5 min
7. Season with salt and pepper

Tips:

- Enhance flavor by adding some crushed red pepper flakes for a spicy touch
- Serve this nourishing soup with a side of sliced avocados for healthy fats

Nutritional Values: Calories: 210, Fat: 10g, Carbs: 6g, Protein: 23g, Sugar: 2g, Sodium: 720mg, Potassium: 580mg, Cholesterol: 65mg

SPICY TOMATO AND EGGPLANT STEW

Preparation Time: 15 min
Cooking Time: 40 min
Mode of Cooking: Stovetop
Servings: 4
Ingredients:

- 1 Tbsp olive oil
- 1 large eggplant, cubed
- 1 onion, diced
- 2 cloves garlic, minced
- 1 chili pepper, diced
- 1 can (28 oz.) diced tomatoes
- 1 tsp smoked paprika
- 1/2 tsp cumin
- Salt and pepper to taste
- 1/4 cup fresh parsley, chopped

Directions:

1. Heat olive oil in a large pot over medium heat
2. Add eggplant, cook until it starts to soften
3. Add onion, garlic, and chili pepper, cook until onion is translucent
4. Stir in diced tomatoes, paprika, and cumin
5. Simmer for 30 min
6. Season with salt and pepper

7. Stir in fresh parsley before serving

Tips:

- Consider roasting the eggplant prior for added depth of flavor
- Accompany with a fresh cucumber salad for a cooling contrast
- Ideal for batch cooking as it stores well in the refrigerator

Nutritional Values: Calories: 180, Fat: 7g, Carbs: 26g, Protein: 5g, Sugar: 13g, Sodium: 560mg, Potassium: 900mg, Cholesterol: 0mg

THAI INSPIRED TURKEY AND SQUASH SOUP

Preparation Time: 20 min.
Cooking Time: 35 min.
Mode of Cooking: Stovetop
Servings: 4
Ingredients:

- 1 lb ground turkey
- 1 medium butternut squash, peeled and cubed
- 1 large carrot, sliced
- 1 red bell pepper, diced
- 4 cups low-sodium chicken broth
- 1 can coconut milk
- 2 Tbsp olive oil
- 3 cloves garlic, minced
- 1 Tbsp fresh ginger, grated
- 1 Tbsp Thai red curry paste
- 1 lime, juiced
- Fresh cilantro, chopped for garnish
- Salt and pepper to taste

Directions:

1. Heat olive oil in a large pot over medium heat
2. Add garlic, ginger, and ground turkey, cook until turkey is browned
3. Stir in red curry paste and cook for 1 minute
4. Add chicken broth, butternut squash, carrot, and bell pepper, bring to a boil
5. Reduce heat and simmer for about 25 minutes until vegetables are tender
6. Stir in coconut milk and lime juice, simmer for another 10 minutes
7. Season with salt and pepper, garnish with fresh cilantro before serving

Tips:

- Experiment with different types of squash for varying flavors and textures
- Add a tablespoon of fish sauce for an extra depth of flavor if desired
- Serve with a side of steamed cauliflower rice for a complete meal

Nutritional Values: Calories: 265, Fat: 14g, Carbs: 15g, Protein: 19g, Sugar: 6g, Sodium: 300 mg, Potassium: 500 mg, Cholesterol: 55 mg

CAULIFLOWER AND SMOKED PAPRIKA STEW

Preparation Time: 15 min.
Cooking Time: 40 min.
Mode of Cooking: Stovetop
Servings: 6
Ingredients:

- 1 large head of cauliflower, cut into florets
- 2 Tbsp smoked paprika
- 1 Tbsp olive oil
- 1 medium onion, chopped
- 2 cloves garlic, minced
- 4 cups vegetable broth
- 1 can diced tomatoes
- 1 Tbsp apple cider vinegar
- Salt and fresh cracked black pepper to taste
- Fresh parsley, chopped for garnish

Directions:

1. In a large pot, heat olive oil over medium heat
2. Add onion and garlic, sauté until onion is translucent
3. Add smoked paprika and stir for about 1 minute until fragrant
4. Add cauliflower, diced tomatoes, and vegetable broth, bring to a boil
5. Reduce heat to low and simmer for about 30 minutes until cauliflower is tender
6. Stir in apple cider vinegar
7. Season with salt and pepper, garnish with fresh parsley before serving

Tips:

- Use roasted cauliflower for a nuttier flavor
- Incorporate a teaspoon of chili flakes for a spicy kick
- Top with toasted almond slices for added crunch and protein

Nutritional Values: Calories: 90, Fat: 3.5g, Carbs: 12g, Protein: 4g, Sugar: 7g, Sodium: 500 mg, Potassium: 300 mg, Cholesterol: 0 mg

HEARTY BEEF AND SWEET POTATO STEW

Preparation Time: 15 min.
Cooking Time: 1 hr.
Mode of Cooking: Stovetop
Servings: 5
Ingredients:

- 1.5 lb beef stew meat, trimmed and cubed
- 2 medium sweet potatoes, peeled and cubed
- 1 Tbsp olive oil
- 1 large onion, diced
- 3 cloves garlic, minced

- 3 cups beef broth
- 1 Tbsp fresh rosemary, chopped
- 1 tsp ground cumin
- Salt and pepper to taste
- Fresh thyme for garnish

Directions:

1. Heat olive oil in a large pot over medium-high heat
2. Brown beef cubes on all sides
3. Add onions and garlic, cook until softened
4. Pour in beef broth and bring to a boil
5. Add sweet potatoes, rosemary, and cumin
6. Reduce heat to low, cover, and simmer for about 45 minutes or until beef is tender
7. Season with salt and pepper, garnish with fresh thyme before serving

Tips:

- Sear the beef in batches to avoid overcrowding and ensure even browning
- Add a splash of balsamic vinegar for a slight tang
- Serve with a side of roasted Brussels sprouts for additional nutrients

Nutritional Values: Calories: 310, Fat: 10g, Carbs: 22g, Protein: 34g, Sugar: 5g, Sodium: 570 mg, Potassium: 600 mg, Cholesterol: 90 mg

MEDITERRANEAN FISH AND VEGETABLE SOUP

Preparation Time: 10 min.
Cooking Time: 25 min.
Mode of Cooking: Stovetop
Servings: 4
Ingredients:

- 1 lb white fish fillets, like cod or tilapia, cut into chunks
- 1 bell pepper, sliced
- 1 zucchini, sliced
- 1 onion, chopped
- 2 cloves garlic, minced
- 3 cups fish or vegetable broth
- 1 can diced tomatoes
- 1 tsp dried oregano
- Olive oil for sautéing
- Salt and black pepper to taste
- Fresh basil, chopped for garnish

Directions:

1. In a large pot, heat olive oil over medium heat
2. Add onion and garlic, sauté until onion is translucent
3. Add bell pepper and zucchini, cook for 2-3 minutes
4. Pour in broth and diced tomatoes, bring to a boil

5. Add fish chunks and oregano, reduce heat to simmer for about 12-15 minutes until fish is cooked through
6. Season with salt and pepper, garnish with fresh basil before serving

Tips:

- Try adding a pinch of saffron for a luxurious flavor and color
- Include a tablespoon of capers for a briny depth
- Accompany with a slice of Whole30 compliant toasted almond bread for dipping

Nutritional Values: Calories: 180, Fat: 5g, Carbs: 10g, Protein: 26g, Sugar: 4g, Sodium: 420 mg, Potassium: 450 mg, Cholesterol: 55 mg

---

SPICY CHICKEN AND KALE SOUP

Preparation Time: 20 min.
Cooking Time: 30 min.
Mode of Cooking: Stovetop
Servings: 6
Ingredients:

- 1 lb chicken breasts, diced
- 1 bunch kale, stems removed and leaves chopped
- 1 Tbsp coconut oil
- 1 onion, diced
- 2 cloves garlic, minced
- 1 jalapeño, seeded and finely chopped
- 4 cups chicken broth
- 1 tsp ground turmeric
- 1 tsp cumin
- Salt and pepper to taste
- Fresh cilantro, chopped for garnish

Directions:

1. Melt coconut oil in a large pot over medium heat
2. Add chicken and brown on all sides
3. Add onion, garlic, and jalapeño, cook until onion is soft
4. Pour in chicken broth and bring to a boil
5. Add kale, turmeric, and cumin
6. Reduce heat to simmer for about 20 minutes or until chicken is cooked and kale is tender
7. Season with salt and pepper, garnish with fresh cilantro before serving

Tips:

- To increase spiciness, include the seeds of jalapeño
- Stir in a squeeze of lemon juice just before serving to enhance flavors
- Complement with a side of roasted butternut squash for a hearty meal

Nutritional Values: Calories: 165, Fat: 4g, Carbs: 8g, Protein: 25g, Sugar: 2g, Sodium: 600 mg, Potassium: 350 mg, Cholesterol: 60 mg

SPICED PUMPKIN & CARROT STEW

Preparation Time: 20 min.

Cooking Time: 35 min.

Mode of Cooking: Stovetop

Servings: 4

Ingredients:

- 1 lb. pumpkin, peeled and cubed
- 1 lb. carrots, peeled and sliced
- 1 large onion, diced
- 3 cloves garlic, minced
- 2 Tbsp olive oil
- 4 cups chicken broth (Whole30 compliant)
- 1 tsp ground cumin
- ½ tsp ground cinnamon
- ¼ tsp ground nutmeg
- Salt and black pepper to taste
- Fresh cilantro, chopped for garnish

Directions:

1. Heat olive oil in a large pot over medium heat
2. Add onions and garlic, sauté until translucent
3. Add pumpkin and carrots, cook for 5 min.
4. Stir in cumin, cinnamon, and nutmeg
5. Pour in chicken broth, bring to boil
6. Reduce heat, simmer until vegetables are tender, about 30 min.
7. Season with salt and black pepper
8. Serve garnished with fresh cilantro

Tips:

- Serve with a squeeze of fresh lime juice for an extra zing
- Pair with a roasted chicken breast for a complete meal
- Make extra to store in the freezer for a quick future meal

Nutritional Values: Calories: 195, Fat: 7g, Carbs: 33g, Protein: 5g, Sugar: 14g, Sodium: 480 mg, Potassium: 960 mg, Cholesterol: 0 mg

BEEF AND BUTTERNUT SQUASH CHILI

Preparation Time: 15 min.

Cooking Time: 1 hr.

Mode of Cooking: Simmer

Servings: 6

Ingredients:

- 1 lb. ground beef
- 1 medium butternut squash, peeled and cubed
- 1 large bell pepper, diced

- 1 onion, chopped
- 2 cloves garlic, minced
- 1 Tbsp olive oil
- 2 cups diced tomatoes (canned, no additives)
- 1 Tbsp chili powder
- 1 tsp smoked paprika
- 1 tsp ground cumin
- Salt and pepper to taste

Directions:

1. Brown ground beef in a large pot over medium heat, drain excess fat
2. Set beef aside
3. In the same pot, heat olive oil
4. Add onion, bell pepper, and garlic, sauté until soft
5. Return beef to pot, add butternut squash and diced tomatoes
6. Stir in chili powder, smoked paprika, and cumin
7. Season with salt and pepper
8. Simmer on low heat until squash is tender, about 45 min.

Tips:

- Top with fresh chopped cilantro before serving
- Can be served over cauliflower rice for a hearty meal
- Store in airtight containers in the fridge for up to 3 days

Nutritional Values: Calories: 290, Fat: 15g, Carbs: 22g, Protein: 17g, Sugar: 7g, Sodium: 350 mg, Potassium: 770 mg, Cholesterol: 50 mg

CHAPTER 6: VEGETABLE-CENTRIC SIDE RECIPES

In the bountiful garden of the Whole30 diet, vegetables not only play the role of humble side dishes but also emerge as vibrant, flavorful stars that can transform your meals and your health. As we focus our forks on these earth-given treasures in Chapter 6, I'm excited to guide you through a world where these side recipes aren't just an afterthought—they're central to enlivening your plate and palatal experience.

Embarking on a culinary adventure with vegetable-centric dishes allows us to explore colors, textures, and flavors in their most natural form. From the crisp crunch of a fresh snap pea to the comforting, earthy softness of roasted root vegetables, each recipe in this chapter is designed to maximize not only the nutritional content but also the sensory enjoyment of eating wholesome foods.

Consider the quiet elegance of a perfectly steamed artichoke, or the robust flair of spiced cauliflower steaks sizzling right out of the oven. These dishes do more than just accompany a main course; they bring balance, variety, and zest, making each meal a festive, sensory celebration. The beauty of focusing on vegetables is not only in their versatility but also in how they support your body's health, enhancing digestion, providing essential nutrients, and offering ample fiber—all core components of the Whole30 approach to well-being.

Moreover, preparing these vegetable-centric sides offers an opportunity to slow down and connect with your food. Each stir, chop, and simmer becomes a step closer to understanding the true essence of eating whole. It's not just about sticking to a diet; it's about crafting a lifestyle that energizes, heals, and satisfies.

As we delve into the recipes in this chapter, remember that each vegetable has a story — from the soil it grew in to the farmer who nurtured it. By choosing to make vegetables a compelling part of your diet, you're not only nurturing your family's health but also participating in a global story of sustainable, conscious eating. Let's celebrate and savor every bite of nature's bounty with joy and creativity, turning these so-called side dishes into heroes of the Whole30 journey.

ROASTED RAINBOW CARROT FRIES

Preparation Time: 10 min.
Cooking Time: 25 min.
Mode of Cooking: Oven Roasting
Servings: 4
Ingredients:

- 1 lb. small rainbow carrots, peeled and cut into thin sticks
- 2 Tbsp olive oil
- 1 tsp smoked paprika
- Salt to taste
- Fresh thyme leaves, for garnish

Directions:

1. Preheat oven to 425°F (220°C)
2. Toss carrots with olive oil, smoked paprika, and salt
3. Spread evenly on a baking sheet
4. Roast until crispy and tender, turning once
5. Garnish with fresh thyme leaves before serving

Tips:

- Great with a homemade aioli dipping sauce
- Store in an airtight container for up to three days in the refrigerator if needed

Nutritional Values: Calories: 120, Fat: 7g, Carbs: 14g, Protein: 1g, Sugar: 7g, Sodium: 210 mg, Potassium: 360 mg, Cholesterol: 0 mg

SPICY CILANTRO-LIME CAULIFLOWER RICE

Preparation Time: 5 min.
Cooking Time: 15 min.
Mode of Cooking: Stir-Frying
Servings: 4
Ingredients:

- 1 medium head of cauliflower, riced
- 2 Tbsp coconut oil
- 1/2 cup fresh cilantro, chopped
- Zest and juice of one lime
- 1/2 tsp chili flakes
- Salt to taste

Directions:

1. Heat coconut oil over medium heat in a large skillet
2. Add riced cauliflower; stir-fry until slightly golden, about 8 min.
3. Stir in cilantro, lime zest, lime juice, chili flakes, and salt
4. Cook for an additional 2 min.

Tips:

- Can be served hot or cold
- Pairs wonderfully with grilled fish or chicken
- Add diced avocado for extra richness

Nutritional Values: Calories: 104, Fat: 7g, Carbs: 10g, Protein: 3g, Sugar: 4g, Sodium: 120 mg, Potassium: 430 mg, Cholesterol: 0 mg

GARLIC-THYME STEAMED GREEN BEANS

Preparation Time: 10 min.
Cooking Time: 7 min.
Mode of Cooking: Steaming
Servings: 5
Ingredients:

- 1 lb. fresh green beans, trimmed
- 3 cloves garlic, finely minced
- 2 Tbsp ghee
- 1 tsp fresh thyme leaves
- Salt and pepper to taste

Directions:

1. Bring water to a boil in a pot fitted with a steaming basket
2. Place green beans and garlic in the basket
3. Cover and steam until beans are tender, about 7 min.
4. Toss steamed beans with ghee, thyme, salt, and pepper

Tips:

- Ghee can be substituted with olive oil for a lighter version
- Perfect addition to any meat-centric main course
- Garlic can be adjusted according to taste preferences

Nutritional Values: Calories: 80, Fat: 5g, Carbs: 8g, Protein: 2g, Sugar: 2g, Sodium: 150 mg, Potassium: 230 mg, Cholesterol: 15 mg

ROASTED SPAGHETTI SQUASH WITH SAGE

Preparation Time: 10 min.
Cooking Time: 40 min.
Mode of Cooking: Oven Roasting
Servings: 6
Ingredients:

- 1 large spaghetti squash, halved and seeds removed
- 3 Tbsp olive oil
- 2 Tbsp fresh sage, finely chopped
- Salt and pepper to taste

Directions:

1. Preheat oven to 400°F (200°C)
2. Drizzle each half of the squash with olive oil and season with salt and pepper
3. Sprinkle chopped sage over the squash
4. Place cut side down on a baking sheet
5. Roast until tender, about 40 min.
6. Scrape the squash with a fork to create strands

Tips:

- Squash can be stuffed with additional ingredients like pine nuts or sun-dried tomatoes for variety
- Leftover squash keeps well in the refrigerator and makes a great addition to salads or as a pasta substitute

Nutritional Values: Calories: 90, Fat: 7g, Carbs: 7g, Protein: 1g, Sugar: 3g, Sodium: 260 mg, Potassium: 150 mg, Cholesterol: 0 mg

SMOKEY CHARRED BRUSSELS SPROUTS

Preparation Time: 5 min.
Cooking Time: 10 min.
Mode of Cooking: Grilling
Servings: 4
Ingredients:

- 1 lb. Brussels sprouts, halved
- 2 Tbsp avocado oil
- 1 tsp smoked salt
- 1/4 tsp ground black pepper
- Lemon wedges, for serving

Directions:

1. Preheat grill to medium-high heat

2. Toss Brussels sprouts with avocado oil, smoked salt, and pepper
3. Grill cut side down without stirring until charred, about 5 to 7 min.
4. Serve with lemon wedges

Tips:

- Sprouts can also be roasted in the oven at 425°F (220°C) if grilling isn't an option
- Adjust the seasoning with smoked paprika for added smokiness
- Serve immediately for best texture

Nutritional Values: Calories: 108, Fat: 7g, Carbs: 10g, Protein: 4g, Sugar: 2g, Sodium: 480 mg, Potassium: 441 mg, Cholesterol: 0 mg

---

ROASTED RAINBOW CARROTS WITH FRESH THYME

Preparation Time: 10 min.
Cooking Time: 25 min.
Mode of Cooking: Roasting
Servings: 4
Ingredients:

- 1 lb. multicolored carrots, peeled and halved lengthwise
- 2 Tbsp extra virgin olive oil
- 1 tsp fresh thyme, minced
- Sea salt, to taste
- Freshly ground black pepper, to taste

Directions:

1. Preheat oven to 425°F (220°C)
2. Toss the carrots with olive oil, thyme, salt, and pepper on a baking sheet
3. Spread in a single layer and roast in the oven until tender and caramelized, about 25 min.

Tips:

- Serve immediately for best flavor
- Can be paired excellently with a lean protein dish for a balanced meal

Nutritional Values: Calories: 120, Fat: 7g, Carbs: 14g, Protein: 1g, Sugar: 7g, Sodium: 86 mg, Potassium: 354 mg, Cholesterol: 0 mg

---

SAUTÉED SWISS CHARD WITH GARLIC AND LEMON ZEST

Preparation Time: 5 min.
Cooking Time: 10 min.
Mode of Cooking: Sautéing
Servings: 4
Ingredients:

- 1 bunch Swiss chard, stems removed and leaves chopped
- 2 Tbsp coconut oil
- 2 cloves garlic, minced
- Zest of 1 lemon
- Sea salt, to taste
- Freshly ground black pepper, to taste

Directions:

1. Heat coconut oil in a large skillet over medium heat

2. Add garlic and cook until fragrant, about 1 min.

3. Add Swiss chard leaves and sauté until wilted, about 5 min.

4. Stir in lemon zest, salt, and pepper and cook for an additional 1 min.

Tips:

- Lemon zest adds a fresh, zesty flavor that complements the earthy tones of Swiss chard
- This side dish is perfect alongside a fish or poultry main course

Nutritional Values: Calories: 77, Fat: 7g, Carbs: 3g, Protein: 1g, Sugar: 1g, Sodium: 213 mg, Potassium: 296 mg, Cholesterol: 0 mg

---

CUMIN-SPICED CAULIFLOWER STEAKS

Preparation Time: 10 min.
Cooking Time: 20 min.
Mode of Cooking: Roasting
Servings: 4
Ingredients:

- 1 large head cauliflower, sliced into 1" thick steaks
- 3 Tbsp olive oil
- 2 tsp ground cumin
- 1 tsp paprika
- Sea salt, to taste
- Freshly ground black pepper, to taste

Directions:

1. Preheat oven to 400°F (204°C)

2. In a small bowl, mix olive oil, cumin, paprika, salt, and pepper

3. Brush each cauliflower steak with the mixture

4. Place on a baking sheet and roast until golden and tender, about 20 min.

Tips:

- For added crispness, broil for 2-3 min. at the end of roasting
- Serve with a drizzle of tahini for a creamy contrast

Nutritional Values: Calories: 164, Fat: 14g, Carbs: 9g, Protein: 3g, Sugar: 3g, Sodium: 34 mg, Potassium: 470 mg, Cholesterol: 0 mg

---

SPICY ROASTED OKRA WITH CILANTRO

Preparation Time: 10 min.
Cooking Time: 20 min.
Mode of Cooking: Roasting
Servings: 4
Ingredients:

- 1 lb. okra, ends trimmed and sliced in half lengthwise
- 2 Tbsp avocado oil
- 1 tsp chili powder

- 1 tsp garlic powder
- 1/2 tsp sea salt
- 1/4 cup fresh cilantro, chopped

Directions:

1. Preheat oven to 425°F (220°C)
2. In a bowl, toss okra with avocado oil, chili powder, garlic powder, and salt
3. Spread on a baking sheet in a single layer and roast until crispy, about 20 min.
4. Remove from oven and toss with fresh cilantro

Tips:

- Roasting okra minimizes the slime-factor
- The cilantro adds a refreshing touch to balance the spice

Nutritional Values: Calories: 103, Fat: 7g, Carbs: 10g, Protein: 2g, Sugar: 2g, Sodium: 299 mg, Potassium: 360 mg, Cholesterol: 0 mg

BALSAMIC BRUSSELS SPROUTS WITH CRISPY PROSCIUTTO

Preparation Time: 15 min.
Cooking Time: 25 min.
Mode of Cooking: Roasting
Servings: 4
Ingredients:

- 1.5 lbs Brussels sprouts, trimmed and halved
- 2 Tbsp olive oil
- 4 slices prosciutto, chopped
- 3 Tbsp balsamic vinegar
- Sea salt, to taste
- Freshly ground black pepper, to taste

Directions:

1. Preheat oven to 400°F (204°C)
2. Toss Brussels sprouts with olive oil, salt, and pepper
3. Spread on a baking sheet and roast for 20 min.
4. Add prosciutto and balsamic vinegar and roast for another 5 min.

Tips:

- The prosciutto adds a savory depth
- The balsamic vinegar provides a touch of sweetness and acidity

Nutritional Values: Calories: 194, Fat: 11g, Carbs: 18g, Protein: 7g, Sugar: 5g, Sodium: 320 mg, Potassium: 668 mg, Cholesterol: 12 mg

SMOKY CHARRED CAULIFLOWER STEAKS

Preparation Time: 10 min
Cooking Time: 25 min
Mode of Cooking: Roasting
Servings: 4
Ingredients:

- 1 large head of cauliflower, leaves removed and sliced into thick steaks
- 3 Tbsp olive oil
- 1 tsp smoked paprika
- 1 tsp garlic powder
- 1/2 tsp ground cumin
- Salt and pepper to taste
- Fresh parsley, chopped for garnish

Directions:

1. Preheat oven to 425°F (220°C)
2. In a small bowl, combine olive oil, smoked paprika, garlic powder, cumin, salt, and pepper
3. Brush each cauliflower steak with the oil mixture
4. Place on a baking sheet and roast in the oven for about 25 min, turning halfway through, until tender and charred on the edges
5. Garnish with chopped parsley before serving

Tips:

- Option to sprinkle with lemon zest for a fresh twist
- Serve alongside a fresh garden salad for a complete meal

Nutritional Values: Calories: 120, Fat: 7g, Carbs: 10g, Protein: 3g, Sugar: 4g, Sodium: 30 mg, Potassium: 430 mg, Cholesterol: 0 mg

HERBED ZUCCHINI RIBBON SALAD

Preparation Time: 15 min
Cooking Time: none
Mode of Cooking: No Cooking
Servings: 4
Ingredients:

- 4 medium zucchini, cut into thin ribbons using a vegetable peeler
- 2 Tbsp extra virgin olive oil
- 1 Tbsp lemon juice
- 1/4 cup chopped fresh basil
- 1/4 cup chopped fresh mint
- Salt and pepper to taste
- 1/4 tsp red pepper flakes

Directions:

1. Combine zucchini ribbons, olive oil, lemon juice, basil, mint, salt, pepper, and red pepper flakes in a large bowl
2. Toss gently to coat the zucchini evenly with the dressing and herbs
3. Allow to marinate for about 10 min before serving to enhance flavors

Tips:

- Great paired with grilled fish or chicken
- Store in the refrigerator and consume within a day for best texture

Nutritional Values: Calories: 90, Fat: 7g, Carbs: 6g, Protein: 2g, Sugar: 3g, Sodium: 20 mg, Potassium: 400 mg, Cholesterol: 0 mg

CHAPTER 7: MAIN COURSES FEATURING RED MEAT

Embracing the Whole30 journey brings an exciting chapter into your life, especially when it involves red meat—a staple that's both satisfying and nourishing. While some dietary plans restrict the joy of a juicy steak or a tender roast, Whole30 transforms this luxury into a cornerstone of healthful eating. With nuanced flavors and hearty textures, red meat dishes are designed not only to satisfy your culinary cravings but also to fortify your body's wellness.

In this chapter, we explore the versatile world of red meat, showing how it can be a catalyst for both energy and health improvement. I will guide you through selecting the best cuts, focusing on quality and sustainability, and I will share secrets to cooking methods that enhance flavor without adding unhealthy extras. From the rich, slow-cooked braises that fill your home with inviting aromas to quick, vibrant stir-fries that keep weeknights exciting, each recipe is crafted to ensure you maintain your Whole30 commitment with enthusiasm.

Imagine sitting down to a meal with your family where the centerpiece is a beautifully cooked piece of beef, its flavors heightened by spices and herbs that comply with the Whole30 guidelines. These moments are not just about feeding the body but about enriching the soul and gathering around wholesome food that promotes health and happiness.

Moreover, this chapter also addresses common concerns such as making the most of your budget while choosing the best quality meats and managing portion sizes to align with a healthy diet. As you turn these pages, you'll find that each recipe is more than just a set of instructions; it's a doorway to a more vibrant life, proving that health-oriented eating does not have to compromise flavor.

Join me in turning every meal into an opportunity for renewal and joy, with dishes that energize and inspire. By the end of this chapter, you'll see that Whole30 friendly main courses featuring red meat are not only about adhering to a set of diet rules but about reviving a love for deep, satisfying, and healthful eating.

GRASS-FED BEEF AND SWEET POTATO SKILLET

Preparation Time: 20 min.
Cooking Time: 35 min.
Mode of Cooking: Sautéing
Servings: 4
Ingredients:

- 1.5 lb. grass-fed ground beef
- 1 large sweet potato, peeled and cubed
- 1 red bell pepper, diced
- 1 medium onion, diced
- 2 cloves garlic, minced
- 2 Tbsp olive oil
- 1 tsp smoked paprika
- 1 tsp ground cumin
- Salt and pepper to taste
- Fresh parsley, chopped for garnish

Directions:

1. Heat olive oil in a large skillet over medium heat
2. Add onion and garlic, sauté until translucent
3. Add ground beef, cook until browned

4. Stir in sweet potato, bell pepper, smoked paprika, and cumin
5. Cover and cook until sweet potatoes are tender, stirring occasionally
6. Season with salt and pepper
7. Garnish with fresh parsley before serving

Tips:

- Serve with a side of steamed green beans for a complete meal
- Use freshly ground spices for enhanced flavor
- Garnish with avocado slices for added creaminess and nutrients

Nutritional Values: Calories: 410, Fat: 22g, Carbs: 28g, Protein: 26g, Sugar: 6g, Sodium: 85 mg, Potassium: 750 mg, Cholesterol: 80 mg

---

ROSEMARY-THYME LAMB CHOPS

Preparation Time: 15 min.
Cooking Time: 15 min.
Mode of Cooking: Grilling
Servings: 4
Ingredients:

- 8 lamb chops
- 3 Tbsp olive oil
- 1 Tbsp fresh rosemary, finely chopped
- 1 Tbsp fresh thyme, finely chopped
- 2 cloves garlic, minced
- Salt and pepper to taste

Directions:

1. Preheat grill to high (around 400°F or 204°C)
2. Mix olive oil, rosemary, thyme, and garlic in a bowl to create a marinade
3. Season lamb chops with salt and pepper, then coat evenly with the marinade
4. Grill lamb chops for about 7 minutes per side or until desired doneness is achieved

Tips:

- Serve with a fresh cucumber salad for a refreshing side
- Let the lamb chops rest for 5 minutes after grilling to ensure juiciness
- Marinate for at least 30 minutes before grilling to enhance flavor infusion

Nutritional Values: Calories: 380, Fat: 26g, Carbs: 0g, Protein: 34g, Sugar: 0g, Sodium: 75 mg, Potassium: 499 mg, Cholesterol: 105 mg

---

SPICED BALSAMIC VENISON STEAK

Preparation Time: 25 min.
Cooking Time: 10 min.
Mode of Cooking: Pan-searing
Servings: 4
Ingredients:

- 4 venison steaks, about 1 inch thick
- 3 Tbsp balsamic vinegar

- 2 Tbsp olive oil
- 1 tsp ground coriander
- 1 tsp ground cinnamon
- Salt and pepper to taste
- Fresh thyme for garnish

Directions:

1. Combine balsamic vinegar, olive oil, coriander, and cinnamon in a bowl to make a marinade
2. Season venison steaks with salt and pepper and marinate for at least 20 minutes
3. Heat a skillet to medium-high and sear steaks for about 5 minutes per side or until done to your liking
4. Garnish with fresh thyme

Tips:

- Pair with roasted root vegetables for a hearty meal
- Marinating the venison overnight will deepen the flavors
- Ensure your skillet is very hot before adding the steaks to achieve a good sear

Nutritional Values: Calories: 320, Fat: 12g, Carbs: 3g, Protein: 46g, Sugar: 1g, Sodium: 60 mg, Potassium: 610 mg, Cholesterol: 120 mg

CUMIN-GARLIC RUBBED BISON RIBEYE

Preparation Time: 15 min.
Cooking Time: 8 min.
Mode of Cooking: Grilling
Servings: 2
Ingredients:

- 2 bison ribeye steaks
- 2 Tbsp olive oil
- 2 tsp ground cumin
- 3 cloves garlic, minced
- Salt and pepper to taste

Directions:

1. Preheat grill to medium-high (about 375°F or 190°C)
2. Mix olive oil, cumin, and minced garlic to form a rub
3. Season steaks with salt and pepper, then apply the rub evenly to both sides
4. Grill steaks for about 4 minutes per side or until they reach desired doneness

Tips:

- Accompany with a spinach and strawberry salad for a meal rich in iron and antioxidants
- Let the steaks rest for a few minutes after grilling to help retain the juices
- For a smokier flavor, add a few wood chips to your grill

Nutritional Values: Calories: 380, Fat: 22g, Carbs: 1g, Protein: 40g, Sugar: 0g, Sodium: 65 mg, Potassium: 540 mg, Cholesterol: 90 mg

HERBED FLANK STEAK WITH CHIMICHURRI

Preparation Time: 20 min.
Cooking Time: 10 min.
Mode of Cooking: Broiling
Servings: 4
Ingredients:

- 1 lb. flank steak
- 1/4 cup olive oil
- 1/4 cup fresh parsley, finely chopped
- 1/4 cup fresh cilantro, finely chopped
- 3 Tbsp red wine vinegar
- 2 Tbsp fresh oregano, finely chopped
- 3 cloves garlic, minced
- Salt and pepper to taste

Directions:

1. Combine olive oil, parsley, cilantro, red wine vinegar, oregano, and garlic to make chimichurri
2. Season flank steak with salt and pepper
3. Preheat broiler to high and broil steak for 5 minutes on each side or until desired doneness is achieved
4. Slice steak thinly against the grain and serve with chimichurri drizzled over top

Tips:

- Serve with roasted sweet potatoes for added nutrition
- Let the steak marinate with a bit of chimichurri for an hour before cooking for enhanced flavor
- Slice the steak thinly to ensure tenderness

Nutritional Values: Calories: 300, Fat: 18g, Carbs: 2g, Protein: 30g, Sugar: 0g, Sodium: 70 mg, Potassium: 480 mg, Cholesterol: 70 mg

HERB-CRUSTED RACK OF LAMB WITH GARLIC-INFUSED OLIVE OIL

Preparation Time: 20 min.
Cooking Time: 35 min.
Mode of Cooking: Roasting
Servings: 4
Ingredients:

- 2 lb. rack of lamb, frenched
- 3 Tbsp fresh rosemary, finely chopped
- 3 Tbsp fresh thyme, finely chopped
- 2 cloves garlic, minced
- 1 Tbsp olive oil
- Sea salt to taste
- Freshly ground black pepper to taste

Directions:

1. Preheat oven to 400°F (204°C)
2. In a small bowl, combine rosemary, thyme, garlic, salt, and pepper with olive oil to form a paste

3. Pat the rack of lamb dry and rub the herb paste evenly over the meat
4. Place the lamb in a roasting pan and roast in the preheated oven for 25-30 min. for medium-rare or until desired doneness
5. Let rest for 10 min. before slicing

Tips:
- Use a meat thermometer to ensure perfect doneness
- Letting the lamb rest before slicing keeps it juicy and flavorful

Nutritional Values: Calories: 410, Fat: 34g, Carbs: 0g, Protein: 24g, Sugar: 0g, Sodium: 105 mg, Potassium: 330 mg, Cholesterol: 105 mg

---

SPICED BEEF TENDERLOIN WITH CAULIFLOWER RICE PILAF

Preparation Time: 15 min.
Cooking Time: 40 min.
Mode of Cooking: Searing and Baking
Servings: 6
Ingredients:
- 2 lb. beef tenderloin
- 1 Tbsp smoked paprika
- 1 tsp cumin
- 1 tsp coriander
- ½ tsp black pepper
- ½ tsp sea salt
- 2 Tbsp coconut oil
- 3 cups riced cauliflower
- 1 cup diced bell peppers
- ½ cup diced onions
- 2 cloves garlic, minced
- 1 Tbsp olive oil
- Fresh parsley, chopped for garnish

Directions:
1. Preheat oven to 375°F (190°C)
2. Mix paprika, cumin, coriander, salt, and pepper together and rub evenly over beef tenderloin
3. Heat coconut oil in a skillet over high heat and sear tenderloin on all sides
4. Transfer to a baking dish and roast in preheated oven for 30 min. or until desired doneness
5. While beef roasts, heat olive oil in a pan, add onions, bell peppers, and garlic, sauté until soft
6. Add riced cauliflower and cook for 5 min., stirring frequently
7. Serve beef sliced with cauliflower rice pilaf garnished with parsley

Tips:
- Let the tenderloin rest before slicing to retain juices
- Cauliflower rice can be flavored with additional herbs if desired

Nutritional Values: Calories: 398, Fat: 23g, Carbs: 9g, Protein: 38g, Sugar: 4g, Sodium: 212 mg, Potassium: 637 mg, Cholesterol: 112 mg

GRILLED FLANK STEAK WITH CHIMICHURRI SAUCE

Preparation Time: 15 min.
Cooking Time: 10 min.
Mode of Cooking: Grilling
Servings: 4
Ingredients:

- 1½ lb. flank steak
- Sea salt to taste
- Freshly ground black pepper to taste
- 1 cup fresh parsley
- ¼ cup fresh oregano leaves
- 2 cloves garlic
- 2 Tbsp red wine vinegar
- ½ cup olive oil
- 1 tsp red pepper flakes

Directions:

1. Preheat grill to high heat
2. Season flank steak with salt and pepper
3. Grill steak for 5 min. on each side or until desired level of doneness
4. For chimichurri, blend parsley, oregano, garlic, vinegar, olive oil, and red pepper flakes until smooth in a food processor
5. Serve steak sliced with chimichurri sauce drizzled over the top

Tips:

- Chimichurri sauce can be made in advance and stored in the refrigerator
- Grill additional vegetables as a healthy side

Nutritional Values: Calories: 487, Fat: 37g, Carbs: 3g, Protein: 34g, Sugar: 0g, Sodium: 124 mg, Potassium: 524 mg, Cholesterol: 90 mg

BALSAMIC GLAZED FILET MIGNON WITH ROASTED ASPARAGUS

Preparation Time: 10 min.
Cooking Time: 25 min.
Mode of Cooking: Pan-searing and Roasting
Servings: 4
Ingredients:

- 4 filet mignon steaks, 6 oz. each
- 2 Tbsp balsamic vinegar
- 1 Tbsp olive oil
- 1 tsp mustard
- Sea salt to taste
- Freshly ground black pepper to taste
- 1 lb. asparagus, trimmed
- 1 Tbsp coconut oil

Directions:

1. Preheat oven to 425°F (218°C)

2. In a small bowl, mix balsamic vinegar, olive oil, mustard, salt, and pepper to create glaze

3. Heat coconut oil in a skillet over medium-high heat, sear steaks for 2 min. on each side

4. Brush steaks with glaze and transfer to preheated oven, roast alongside asparagus for about 10 min. or until desired doneness

5. Serve steaks with roasted asparagus

Tips:

- Brush steaks with balsamic glaze multiple times while roasting for a more robust flavor

- Asparagus can be seasoned with lemon zest for an added zing

Nutritional Values: Calories: 398, Fat: 23g, Carbs: 5g, Protein: 39g, Sugar: 3g, Sodium: 82 mg, Potassium: 648 mg, Cholesterol: 134 mg

ROSEMARY-SCENTED VENISON LOIN WITH ROASTED ROOT VEGETABLES

Preparation Time: 20 min.
Cooking Time: 45 min.
Mode of Cooking: Roasting
Servings: 6
Ingredients:

- 2 lb. venison loin

- 3 Tbsp fresh rosemary, minced

- 2 cloves garlic, minced

- 1 Tbsp olive oil

- Sea salt to taste

- Freshly ground black pepper to taste

- 2 cups diced carrots

- 2 cups diced parsnips

- 2 cups diced sweet potatoes

- 1 Tbsp coconut oil, melted

Directions:

1. Preheat oven to 375°F (190°C)

2. Mix rosemary, garlic, olive oil, salt, and pepper in a small bowl and rub over venison loin

3. Place loin in a roasting pan

4. In a separate bowl, toss carrots, parsnips, and sweet potatoes with melted coconut oil and season with salt and pepper

5. Scatter vegetables around venison in the roasting pan

6. Roast in preheated oven for approximately 40 min., or until venison is cooked to desired doneness and vegetables are tender

7. Serve venison sliced with a side of roasted root vegetables

Tips:

- Let venison rest before slicing to enhance juiciness

- Experiment with different root vegetables like turnips or beets for variety

Nutritional Values: Calories: 354, Fat: 12g, Carbs: 25g, Protein: 35g, Sugar: 7g, Sodium: 79 mg, Potassium: 891 mg, Cholesterol: 128 mg

GRASS-FED BEEF TENDERLOIN WITH ROSEMARY-THYME CRUST

Preparation Time: 20 min.
Cooking Time: 40 min.
Mode of Cooking: Roasting
Servings: 4
Ingredients:

- 2 lb. grass-fed beef tenderloin
- 2 Tbsp fresh rosemary, finely chopped
- 2 Tbsp fresh thyme, finely chopped
- 3 cloves garlic, minced
- 2 Tbsp olive oil
- 1 tsp sea salt
- ½ tsp freshly ground black pepper

Directions:

1. Preheat oven to 400°F (204°C)
2. Combine rosemary, thyme, garlic, olive oil, salt, and pepper in a small bowl
3. Rub the herb mixture evenly over the entire surface of the beef tenderloin
4. Place tenderloin in a roasting pan and roast in the preheated oven for 40 min., or until the meat reaches an internal temperature of 135°F (57°C) for medium-rare
5. Remove from oven, tent with foil, and let rest for 10 min. before slicing

Tips:

- Let the meat rest to redistribute the juices for optimal tenderness
- Slice thinly against the grain to enhance tenderness and flavor

Nutritional Values: Calories: 380, Fat: 25g, Carbs: 1g, Protein: 35g, Sugar: 0g, Sodium: 620 mg, Potassium: 550 mg, Cholesterol: 105 mg

SPICED LAMB SKEWERS WITH MINT CHIMICHURRI

Preparation Time: 30 min.
Cooking Time: 10 min.
Mode of Cooking: Grilling
Servings: 4
Ingredients:

- 1 lb. lamb leg, trimmed and cut into 1-inch cubes
- 2 tsp smoked paprika
- 1 tsp cumin
- 1 tsp sea salt
- ½ tsp black pepper
- 2 Tbsp olive oil
- For the chimichurri: 1 cup fresh mint leaves
- 2 cloves garlic, minced

- 1 jalapeno, seeded and finely chopped
- 3 Tbsp olive oil
- 1 Tbsp apple cider vinegar
- 1 tsp sea salt

Directions:

1. Combine lamb, paprika, cumin, salt, pepper, and olive oil in a bowl, mix well and thread onto skewers
2. Preheat grill to medium-high heat and grill skewers for about 10 min., turning occasionally until browned and cooked to desired doneness
3. For chimichurri, blend mint, garlic, jalapeno, olive oil, vinegar, and salt until smooth
4. Serve skewers drizzled with mint chimichurri

Tips:

- Use metal skewers to avoid burning common with wooden skewers
- Serve with a side of grilled vegetables for a complete meal
- Chimichurri can be made ahead and stored in an airtight container in the refrigerator for up to a week

Nutritional Values: Calories: 295, Fat: 20g, Carbs: 5g, Protein: 23g, Sugar: 0g, Sodium: 680 mg, Potassium: 370 mg, Cholesterol: 90 mg

CHAPTER 8: DISHES FEATURING PORK

As we delve into the succulent world of pork on our Whole30 journey, it becomes clear that this versatile ingredient can transform your meal times from routine to remarkable. Often misunderstood due to its rich fat content, pork, when sourced correctly and prepared thoughtfully, can be a profound centerpiece for nutritious family dining. Each recipe in this chapter has been crafted to elevate this humble meat, ensuring that you derive both maximum flavor and health benefits.

Pork's culinary flexibility allows us to explore a range of recipes that promise to keep your taste buds tantalized while staunchly sticking to the Whole30 guidelines. Whether it's a slow-cooked pork shoulder that falls off the fork, invigorated with herbs and spices, or tender pork chops perfectly seared to retain their juiciness, you'll find dishes here that might just become your new family favorites.

The beauty of pork lies in its ability to absorb flavors, making it an excellent candidate for a host of seasonings — from the bold and piquant to the subtle and sweet. In this chapter, we invite you to experience pork in ways you may never have. Imagine starting a comforting Sunday with a spicy pork hash, or ending a busy weekday with a pork stir-fry that brings a splash of bright vegetables and savory sauces to your dinner table.

Moreover, embracing pork in your Whole30 diet isn't just about broadening your culinary horizons; it's about crafting meals that keep you committed to your health goals. Each dish is designed to ensure that you stay fueled and satisfied, reducing the temptations that often creep in during a transformative diet phase. Through these recipes, you'll discover that maintaining a healthful lifestyle does not only depend on what you can't eat but thrives on the delicious meals you can.

So, whether you're a long-time pork enthusiast or a newcomer ready to transform your dietary habits, this chapter promises a treasure trove of dishes that respect the integrity of the Whole30 program and cater to the festive, yet health-conscious, spirit of any familial table.

PULLED PORK WITH SMOKY DRY RUB

Preparation Time: 20 min.
Cooking Time: 8 hr.
Mode of Cooking: Slow Cooking
Servings: 6
Ingredients:

- 3 lb. pork shoulder
- 1 Tbsp smoked paprika
- 2 tsp garlic powder
- 2 tsp onion powder
- 1 tsp ground cumin
- 1 tsp dried oregano
- 1 tsp sea salt
- 1 tsp cracked black pepper
- ½ cup water

Directions:

1. Mix smoked paprika, garlic powder, onion powder, ground cumin, dried oregano, sea salt, and cracked black pepper to create the dry rub

2. Coat the pork shoulder evenly with the dry rub

3. Place the seasoned pork in a slow cooker and add water

4. Cook on low for 8 hr. or until the pork is tender and shreds easily with a fork

Tips:
- Use two forks to shred the pork for more texture control
- If preferred, let the pork rest for 10 min. before shredding to retain more juices

Nutritional Values: Calories: 330, Fat: 20g, Carbs: 2g, Protein: 33g, Sugar: 0g, Sodium: 590 mg, Potassium: 503 mg, Cholesterol: 107 mg

---

SPICED PORK TENDERLOIN WITH APPLE-FENNEL SALAD

Preparation Time: 15 min.
Cooking Time: 25 min.
Mode of Cooking: Roasting
Servings: 4
Ingredients:
- 1 pork tenderloin, approximately 1 lb.
- 2 Tbsp olive oil
- 1 tsp ground coriander
- 1 tsp fennel seeds
- 1 tsp dried thyme
- salt and pepper to taste
- 2 apples, thinly sliced
- 1 fennel bulb, thinly sliced
- Juice of 1 lemon
- Fresh parsley for garnish

Directions:
1. Preheat oven to 400°F (204°C)
2. Mix ground coriander, fennel seeds, dried thyme, salt, and pepper with olive oil to create a marinade
3. Coat the pork tenderloin in the marinade and place on a roasting tray
4. Roast in the oven for 25 min. until the pork is cooked through
5. Combine sliced apples, fennel, and lemon juice to make the salad
6. Serve the pork sliced with the apple-fennel salad on the side

Tips:
- Let pork rest for 5 min. after roasting before slicing to retain moisture
- For a crisper salad, add lemon juice just before serving

Nutritional Values: Calories: 296, Fat: 14g, Carbs: 17g, Protein: 27g, Sugar: 10g, Sodium: 67 mg, Potassium: 673 mg, Cholesterol: 83 mg

---

PORK AND SWEET POTATO STEW

Preparation Time: 20 min.
Cooking Time: 6 hr.
Mode of Cooking: Slow Cooking
Servings: 5
Ingredients:
- 2 lb. pork loin, cut into chunks
- 3 medium sweet potatoes, peeled and cubed

- 1 large onion, chopped
- 3 cloves garlic, minced
- 1 tsp paprika
- 1 tsp dried rosemary
- 4 cups chicken stock (Whole30 compliant)
- Salt and pepper to taste
- Fresh cilantro for garnish

Directions:

1. Place pork loin, sweet potatoes, onion, garlic, paprika, dried rosemary, salt, and pepper in a slow cooker
2. Pour in chicken stock and ensure the ingredients are well submerged
3. Cook on low for 6 hr. until pork is tender and sweet potatoes are soft
4. Serve hot garnished with fresh cilantro

Tips:

- To thicken the stew, mash some of the sweet potatoes and stir back into the stew
- Adjust seasoning before serving to enhance flavors

Nutritional Values: Calories: 312, Fat: 8g, Carbs: 28g, Protein: 30g, Sugar: 6g, Sodium: 586 mg, Potassium: 1013 mg, Cholesterol: 78 mg

HERB-CRUSTED PORK CHOPS WITH SAUTÉED VEGETABLES

Preparation Time: 10 min.
Cooking Time: 15 min.
Mode of Cooking: Pan Frying
Servings: 4
Ingredients:

- 4 pork chops, bone-in
- 1 Tbsp dried basil
- 1 Tbsp dried thyme
- 1 Tbsp dried rosemary
- 1 clove garlic, minced
- Salt and pepper to taste
- 2 Tbsp olive oil
- 1 zucchini, sliced
- 1 yellow squash, sliced
- 1 red bell pepper, sliced

Directions:

1. Mix dried basil, thyme, rosemary, minced garlic, salt, and pepper to create a herb crust for the pork chops
2. Heat olive oil in a skillet over medium heat and cook pork chops for approximately 7 min. on each side or until fully cooked
3. In another skillet, sauté zucchini, squash, and red bell pepper until tender
4. Serve pork chops with sautéed vegetables on the side

Tips:

- Pork chops can be covered with a tent of aluminum foil while resting to keep them warm

- Sauté vegetables while pork chops cook to save time

Nutritional Values: Calories: 290, Fat: 16g, Carbs: 8g, Protein: 30g, Sugar: 4g, Sodium: 87 mg, Potassium: 897 mg, Cholesterol: 90 mg

LEMONGRASS GRILLED PORK SKEWERS

Preparation Time: 30 min.
Cooking Time: 10 min.
Mode of Cooking: Grilling
Servings: 4
Ingredients:

- 1 lb. pork tenderloin, cut into 1-inch cubes
- 2 stalks lemongrass, finely minced
- 3 cloves garlic, minced
- 1 inch ginger, grated
- 1 Tbsp fish sauce (Whole30 compliant)
- 1 Tbsp lime juice
- 2 Tbsp olive oil
- Salt to taste
- Fresh mint for garnish

Directions:

1. Marinate pork cubes with lemongrass, garlic, ginger, fish sauce, lime juice, olive oil, and salt for at least 30 min.
2. Thread the marinated pork onto skewers
3. Grill over medium heat for 10 min., turning occasionally, until cooked through
4. Serve hot garnished with fresh mint

Tips:

- For more flavor, marinate the pork overnight
- Serve with a side of cucumber salad for a refreshing touch

Nutritional Values: Calories: 224, Fat: 10g, Carbs: 3g, Protein: 30g, Sugar: 0g, Sodium: 620 mg, Potassium: 563 mg, Cholesterol: 83 mg

PORK LOIN WITH SPICED APPLE COMPOTE

Preparation Time: 15 min
Cooking Time: 1 hr
Mode of Cooking: Roasting
Servings: 4
Ingredients:

- 1 lb pork loin
- 2 green apples, diced
- 1 tsp ground cinnamon
- 1 tsp cloves
- 1 Tbsp fresh ginger, minced
- 2 Tbsp olive oil

- 1 tsp sea salt
- ½ tsp black pepper

Directions:

1. Preheat oven to 375°F (190°C)
2. Rub pork loin with olive oil, salt, and black pepper
3. Place in a roasting pan and roast for 50 min
4. While roasting, combine apples, cinnamon, cloves, and ginger in a saucepan over medium heat
5. Cook until apples are soft and sauce thickens, about 15 min
6. Serve pork sliced with apple compote on the side

Tips:

- Let pork rest for 10 min before slicing to retain juices
- Use tart apples like Granny Smith for a more intense flavor in the compote
- Ginger can be adjusted according to taste preference

Nutritional Values: Calories: 310, Fat: 14g, Carbs: 15g, Protein: 31g, Sugar: 10g, Sodium: 600 mg, Potassium: 500 mg, Cholesterol: 85 mg

---

HERB-CRUSTED PORK TENDERLOIN WITH CAULIFLOWER MASH

Preparation Time: 20 min
Cooking Time: 40 min
Mode of Cooking: Baking
Servings: 4
Ingredients:

- 1 lb pork tenderloin
- 1 Tbsp rosemary, finely chopped
- 1 Tbsp thyme, finely chopped
- 2 garlic cloves, minced
- 2 Tbsp ghee, melted
- 1 head cauliflower, cut into florets
- 1 Tbsp olive oil
- Sea salt and pepper to taste

Directions:

1. Preheat oven to 400°F (204°C)
2. Mix rosemary, thyme, garlic, and ghee
3. Rub mixture over pork tenderloin
4. Place pork on a baking sheet and roast for 35 min
5. Meanwhile, steam cauliflower until tender, about 15 min
6. Mash cauliflower with olive oil, salt, and pepper using a hand blender or masher
7. Serve pork with cauliflower mash on the side

Tips:

- Rub the herbs under and over the pork skin for enhanced flavors
- Cauliflower mash can be enriched with garlic or onion powder for extra taste
- Ensure pork is thoroughly cooked by checking internal temperature reaches 145°F (63°C)

Nutritional Values: Calories: 295, Fat: 17g, Carbs: 8g, Protein: 28g, Sugar: 4g, Sodium: 320 mg, Potassium: 870 mg, Cholesterol: 80 mg

SPICY PORK STIR-FRY WITH BOK CHOY

Preparation Time: 10 min
Cooking Time: 30 min
Mode of Cooking: Stir-Frying
Servings: 4
Ingredients:

- 1 lb pork shoulder, thinly sliced
- 2 cups bok choy, chopped
- 1 red bell pepper, sliced
- 2 Tbsp coconut aminos
- 1 Tbsp fish sauce
- 2 tsp chili paste
- 1 Tbsp coconut oil
- 1 tsp sesame seeds

Directions:

1. Heat coconut oil in a large skillet over medium-high heat
2. Add pork slices and cook until browned, about 8 min
3. Add bell pepper and bok choy, stir for 5 min
4. Mix in coconut aminos, fish sauce, and chili paste
5. Cook until vegetables are tender and pork is cooked through, about 10 min
6. Sprinkle with sesame seeds before serving

Tips:

- To make this dish Whole30 compliant, ensure that the chili paste is free of added sugars
- Adjust the level of chili paste based on spice preferences
- Pork shoulder can be substituted with pork loin for a leaner option

Nutritional Values: Calories: 320, Fat: 18g, Carbs: 10g, Protein: 30g, Sugar: 5g, Sodium: 900 mg, Potassium: 780 mg, Cholesterol: 95 mg

LEMON-GARLIC PORK CHOPS

Preparation Time: 10 min
Cooking Time: 15 min
Mode of Cooking: Grilling
Servings: 4
Ingredients:

- 4 pork chops, bone-in, 1 inch thick
- 2 lemons, juiced and zested
- 4 garlic cloves, minced
- 2 Tbsp olive oil
- 1 tsp dried oregano
- Sea salt and black pepper to taste

Directions:

1. Preheat grill to medium-high heat, about 375°F (190°C)

2. Mix lemon juice, zest, garlic, olive oil, oregano, salt, and pepper

3. Marinate pork chops in lemon-garlic mixture for at least 30 min

4. Grill pork chops for 7 min per side or until internal temperature reaches 145°F (63°C)

Tips:

- Marinate pork chops overnight for deeper flavor infusion

- Squeeze extra lemon over grilled chops before serving for added zest

- Serve with a side of steamed green beans or asparagus for a complete meal

Nutritional Values: Calories: 290, Fat: 16g, Carbs: 6g, Protein: 29g, Sugar: 2g, Sodium: 320 mg, Potassium: 510 mg, Cholesterol: 80 mg

---

SMOKY PORK COLLARD GREENS

Preparation Time: 15 min
Cooking Time: 1 hr 30 min
Mode of Cooking: Simmering
Servings: 6
Ingredients:

- 2 lb pork ribs

- 4 cups collard greens, chopped

- 1 onion, diced

- 3 cups chicken broth

- 1 smoked ham hock

- 2 Tbsp apple cider vinegar

- 1 tsp smoked paprika

- Sea salt and black pepper to taste

Directions:

1. Combine all ingredients except collard greens in a large pot and bring to a boil

2. Reduce heat and simmer for 1 hr

3. Add collard greens and simmer for additional 30 min

4. Remove ham hock and serve hot

Tips:

- Enhance this dish with a splash of hot sauce for extra heat

- Pork ribs can be pre-browned for added depth of flavor

- Apple cider vinegar can be adjusted based on taste preference

Nutritional Values: Calories: 450, Fat: 30g, Carbs: 8g, Protein: 36g, Sugar: 4g, Sodium: 650 mg, Potassium: 690 mg

---

PORK LOIN WITH HERB CRUST

Preparation Time: 20 min.
Cooking Time: 60 min.
Mode of Cooking: Roasting
Servings: 6

Ingredients:

- 2 lb. pork loin
- 1 Tbsp olive oil
- 2 tsp salt
- 1 tsp black pepper
- 1 Tbsp garlic, minced
- 2 Tbsp fresh rosemary, chopped
- 2 Tbsp fresh thyme, chopped
- 2 Tbsp fresh parsley, chopped
- 1 Tbsp lemon zest

Directions:

1. Preheat oven to 375°F (190°C)
2. Pat pork loin dry with paper towels
3. Rub with olive oil, salt, and pepper
4. In a small bowl, combine minced garlic, chopped rosemary, thyme, parsley, and lemon zest
5. Press herb mixture onto the pork loin, coating thoroughly
6. Place in a roasting pan and roast in the oven for about 1 hr. or until the internal temperature reaches 145°F (63°C), basting occasionally with pan juices
7. Remove from oven and let rest for 10 min before slicing

Tips:

- Let the pork rest to ensure juices distribute evenly, enhancing flavor and tenderness
- Serve with a side of steamed green beans and cauliflower mash for a complete Whole30 meal

Nutritional Values: Calories: 310, Fat: 10g, Carbs: 1g, Protein: 50g, Sugar: 0g, Sodium: 700 mg, Potassium: 850 mg, Cholesterol: 150 mg

---

SPICED PORK AND VEGETABLE SKEWERS

Preparation Time: 25 min.
Cooking Time: 15 min.
Mode of Cooking: Grilling
Servings: 4
Ingredients:

- 1½ lb. pork shoulder, cut into 1-inch cubes
- 2 bell peppers, assorted colors, cubed
- 1 large red onion, cubed
- 2 Tbsp olive oil
- 1 tsp smoked paprika
- 1 tsp garlic powder
- 1 tsp ground cumin
- salt and black pepper to taste
- fresh cilantro leaves for garnish

Directions:

1. Thread pork cubes, bell pepper, and onion alternately onto skewers

2. In a small bowl, mix olive oil, smoked paprika, garlic powder, cumin, salt, and pepper

3. Brush mixture over skewers

4. Preheat grill to medium-high (about 375°F (190°C))

5. Grill skewers, turning occasionally, until pork is cooked through and vegetables are slightly charred, about 15 min

Tips:

- Marinate pork cubes in spice mixture for at least 1 hr before skewering to deepen flavors
- Serve with fresh cilantro sprinkled on top for an added burst of freshness

Nutritional Values: Calories: 420, Fat: 26g, Carbs: 10g, Protein: 36g, Sugar: 5g, Sodium: 620 mg, Potassium: 940 mg, Cholesterol: 110 mg

CHAPTER 9: POULTRY DISHES

Welcome to the delightful world of poultry, a versatile centerpiece in the Whole30 diet that promises to rejuvenate your meal plans with flavors and textures that satisfy every palate in the family. Poultry, particularly chicken and turkey, is celebrated not only for its lean protein—which is crucial for muscle repair and growth—but also for its ability to absorb a myriad of flavors from herbs, spices, and marinades, transforming into dishes that can be both comforting and exotic.

Imagine the aroma of a herb-roasted chicken wafting through your house, or the zesty appeal of a spicy turkey chili that brings warmth to a chilly evening. These are just glimpses of what awaits you in this chapter. Poultry dishes, when prepared with Whole30 guidelines, offer a fantastic opportunity to explore creative culinary techniques without compromising your health goals. We'll explore roasting, grilling, slow-cooking, and even poaching—each method bringing out unique aspects of poultry that you may never have savored before.

The beauty of incorporating poultry into your Whole30 journey lies in its simplicity and the endless possibilities it presents. Whether it's a quick sauté on a busy weekday or a leisurely roasted dish over the weekend, chicken and turkey can be tailored to fit your schedule and taste preferences, proving that healthy eating does not have to be tedious or bland.

This chapter is designed not only to introduce you to an array of dishes that will excite your taste buds but also to empower you with the knowledge to choose the best poultry options and prepare them in ways that preserve and enhance their natural goodness. Here, you'll find dishes that can make both an ordinary family dinner feel special and provide impressive options for social gatherings, all the while keeping you aligned with your Whole30 goals.

Let's embark on this journey with enthusiasm and creativity, knowing that each recipe is a stepping stone towards improved health, energy, and enjoyment of life's simplest pleasures—good food shared with loved ones.

CITRUS ZESTED CHICKEN WITH FENNEL

Preparation Time: 20 min.
Cooking Time: 45 min.
Mode of Cooking: Roasting
Servings: 4
Ingredients:

- 1 whole chicken (about 3-4 lb), giblets removed
- 2 Tbsp olive oil
- 1 large fennel bulb, thinly sliced
- 2 oranges, zested and juiced
- 1 lemon, zested and juiced
- 4 cloves garlic, minced
- 2 tsp dried thyme
- Salt and black pepper to taste

Directions:

1. Pat the chicken dry with paper towels
2. In a small bowl, mix olive oil, orange zest, orange juice, lemon zest, lemon juice, garlic, thyme, salt, and pepper
3. Rub the mixture all over the chicken, inside and out
4. Place the chicken in a roasting pan and scatter the sliced fennel around it

5. Roast in the oven preheated to 375°F (190°C) for about 45 min. or until the chicken's internal temperature reaches 165°F (74°C)

6. Let the chicken rest for 10 min. before carving

Tips:

- Use remaining pan juices as a drizzle for extra flavor
- Garnish with fresh fennel fronds for a touch of freshness and visual appeal
- Utilize any leftover citrus fruit for a side salad

Nutritional Values: Calories: 400, Fat: 27g, Carbs: 8g, Protein: 30g, Sugar: 5g, Sodium: 200 mg, Potassium: 400 mg, Cholesterol: 130 mg

---

SPICED TURKEY PATTIES WITH AVOCADO SALSA

Preparation Time: 15 min.
Cooking Time: 10 min.
Mode of Cooking: Grilling
Servings: 4
Ingredients:

- 1 lb ground turkey
- 1 tsp ground cumin
- 1 tsp smoked paprika
- 1/2 tsp ground coriander
- 1 ripe avocado, diced
- 1 small red onion, finely chopped
- 1 jalapeño, seeded and minced
- Juice of 1 lime
- Fresh cilantro, chopped
- Salt and black pepper to taste

Directions:

1. Combine ground turkey with cumin, smoked paprika, coriander, salt, and black pepper
2. Form into 4 patties
3. Grill patties over medium heat for about 5 min. on each side or until fully cooked
4. In a separate bowl, mix diced avocado, red onion, jalapeño, lime juice, and cilantro to create the salsa
5. Serve the grilled patties with the fresh avocado salsa on top

Tips:

- Keep patties moist by not overcooking
- Store leftover salsa in the refrigerator and use as a dip
- Add a drizzle of olive oil to salsa to enhance richness

Nutritional Values: Calories: 290, Fat: 17g, Carbs: 9g, Protein: 26g, Sugar: 2g, Sodium: 70 mg, Potassium: 500 mg, Cholesterol: 80 mg

---

HERBED CHICKEN DRUMSTICKS WITH CAULIFLOWER RICE

Preparation Time: 10 min.
Cooking Time: 40 min.
Mode of Cooking: Baking

Servings: 4

Ingredients:

- 8 chicken drumsticks
- 2 Tbsp coconut oil, melted
- 1 head of cauliflower, grated into 'rice'
- 1 tsp garlic powder
- 1 Tbsp dried rosemary
- 1 Tbsp dried parsley
- Salt and black pepper to taste

Directions:

1. Coat chicken drumsticks with melted coconut oil, garlic powder, rosemary, parsley, salt, and black pepper
2. Arrange drumsticks on a baking tray
3. Spread the grated cauliflower around the chicken in the same tray
4. Bake in preheated oven at 400°F (200°C) for 40 min. or until drumsticks are golden and fully cooked
5. Stir cauliflower rice halfway through to ensure even cooking

Tips:

- Serve with a squeeze of fresh lemon juice for added zest
- Pair with a side of steamed green beans for a full meal
- Cauliflower rice can be spiced further with turmeric for added health benefits and color

Nutritional Values: Calories: 310, Fat: 18g, Carbs: 9g, Protein: 29g, Sugar: 3g, Sodium: 220 mg, Potassium: 530 mg, Cholesterol: 120 mg

LEMON-THYME ROASTED DUCK

Preparation Time: 15 min.
Cooking Time: 2 hr.
Mode of Cooking: Roasting
Servings: 4
Ingredients:

- 1 whole duck (about 5 lb)
- 3 lemons, halved
- 4 sprigs fresh thyme
- 2 Tbsp ghee, melted
- Salt and black pepper to taste

Directions:

1. Rinse the duck and pat dry
2. Stuff the duck cavity with lemon halves and fresh thyme sprigs
3. Brush the outside of the duck with melted ghee and season generously with salt and black pepper
4. Roast in preheated oven at 350°F (175°C) for about 2 hr. or until the skin is crispy and the meat is tender
5. Let the duck rest for 10 min. before carving

Tips:

- Rendered duck fat can be used to roast vegetables for an aromatic side dish
- Carve the duck table-side to impress guests

- Use leftover carcass to make a rich and flavorful broth

Nutritional Values: Calories: 620, Fat: 47g, Carbs: 0g, Protein: 48g, Sugar: 0g, Sodium: 130 mg, Potassium: 590 mg, Cholesterol: 255 mg

SAGE AND ORANGE GLAZED CHICKEN BREASTS

Preparation Time: 15 min.
Cooking Time: 25 min.
Mode of Cooking: Grilling
Servings: 4
Ingredients:
- 4 chicken breasts, boneless and skinless
- 2 oranges, juiced
- 1 Tbsp fresh sage, finely chopped
- 1 Tbsp olive oil
- 1 tsp raw honey (optional, exclude for strict Whole30)
- Salt and black pepper to taste

Directions:
1. Combine orange juice, finely chopped sage, olive oil, optional honey, salt, and black pepper in a bowl to create a marinade
2. Marinate chicken breasts in the mixture for at least 1 hr. in the refrigerator
3. Grill the marinated chicken breasts over medium heat for about 12-15 min. or until fully cooked, basting occasionally with the remaining marinade

Tips:
- Serve with grilled vegetables for a complete meal
- If excluding honey, enhance sweetness naturally with extra orange zest
- Use leftover marinade to drizzle over cooked chicken for extra flavor

Nutritional Values: Calories: 240, Fat: 7g, Carbs: 6g, Protein: 35g, Sugar: 4g (exclude if not using honey), Sodium: 85 mg, Potassium: 610 mg, Cholesterol: 95 mg

CHICKEN PANZANELLA WITH HERB-INFUSED DRESSING

Preparation Time: 20 min.
Cooking Time: 30 min.
Mode of Cooking: Baking
Servings: 4
Ingredients:
- 2 lb boneless, skinless chicken breasts
- 3 cups diced fresh tomatoes
- 2 cups diced cucumbers
- 1 large red onion, thinly sliced
- 4 cloves garlic, minced
- 2 Tbsp fresh basil, chopped
- 2 Tbsp fresh oregano, chopped
- ¼ cup extra virgin olive oil

- 2 Tbsp apple cider vinegar
- Salt and pepper to taste
- 2 Tbsp capers

Directions:

1. Preheat oven to 375°F (190°C)
2. Season chicken breasts with salt and pepper and place on a baking tray
3. Bake for 25-30 min. or until fully cooked
4. Let chicken cool then dice into bite-sized pieces
5. Combine tomatoes, cucumbers, onion, garlic, basil, oregano, and capers in a large bowl
6. Add diced chicken
7. Whisk together olive oil, vinegar, salt, and pepper to create the dressing
8. Pour dressing over the salad and toss to coat evenly

Tips:

- Allow the salad to rest for 10 min. before serving to enhance flavors
- Can be served both warm or chilled
- Leftovers are great for a quick lunch the next day

Nutritional Values: Calories: 340, Fat: 15g, Carbs: 10g, Protein: 40g, Sugar: 6g, Sodium: 200 mg, Potassium: 650 mg, Cholesterol: 100 mg

TURKEY CAULIFLOWER ALOO GOBI

Preparation Time: 15 min.
Cooking Time: 25 min.
Mode of Cooking: Roasting
Servings: 4
Ingredients:

- 1 lb turkey cutlets
- 1 head cauliflower, cut into florets
- 1 large potato, diced
- 1 tsp turmeric
- 1 tsp cumin
- 1 tsp coriander
- 1 tsp smoked paprika
- 2 Tbsp olive oil
- Salt and pepper to taste
- Fresh cilantro, chopped for garnish

Directions:

1. Preheat oven to 400°F (204°C)
2. Toss cauliflower and potato with olive oil, turmeric, cumin, coriander, paprika, salt, and pepper
3. Roast in the oven for 20 min. until vegetables are tender
4. While vegetables roast, heat a skillet over medium high heat and cook turkey cutlets until golden brown on each side, approximately 3-4 min. per side
5. Slice turkey cutlets and serve with spiced cauliflower and potatoes

6. Garnish with fresh cilantro

Tips:
- Use parchment paper on the tray for easy cleanup
- For a spicier version, add a bit of chili powder or fresh jalapeños to the vegetable mix before roasting
- This dish pairs wonderfully with a side of chilled cucumber raita

Nutritional Values: Calories: 280, Fat: 10g, Carbs: 18g, Protein: 30g, Sugar: 4g, Sodium: 95 mg, Potassium: 800 mg, Cholesterol: 70 mg

---

SPICED POMEGRANATE CHICKEN SKEWERS

Preparation Time: 25 min.
Cooking Time: 10 min.
Mode of Cooking: Grilling
Servings: 4
Ingredients:
- 2 lb chicken thigh fillets, cut into chunks
- ¼ cup pomegranate molasses
- 2 Tbsp olive oil
- 1 tsp ground cumin
- 1 tsp smoked paprika
- ½ tsp ground cinnamon
- ½ tsp ground allspice
- Salt to taste
- Wooden skewers, soaked in water for 20 min.

Directions:
1. Whisk together pomegranate molasses, olive oil, cumin, paprika, cinnamon, allspice, and salt to create a marinade
2. Toss chicken chunks in the marinade and let sit for 20 min.
3. Thread marinated chicken onto soaked skewers
4. Preheat grill to medium-high and grill skewers for 5 min. on each side or until fully cooked

Tips:
- Serve with a fresh green salad or steamed vegetables to keep it Whole30 friendly
- If pomegranate molasses is not available, reduce balsamic vinegar mixed with a little orange juice can be used as a substitute
- Remember to keep chicken moist by drizzling some extra virgin olive oil after grilling if needed

Nutritional Values: Calories: 310, Fat: 16g, Carbs: 10g, Protein: 32g, Sugar: 7g, Sodium: 75 mg, Potassium: 400 mg, Cholesterol: 115 mg

---

HERBED LEMON GARLIC GAME HENS

Preparation Time: 15 min.
Cooking Time: 1 hr.
Mode of Cooking: Roasting
Servings: 4
Ingredients:
- 4 Cornish game hens

- 4 cloves garlic, minced
- 2 lemons, one juiced and one cut into wedges
- ¼ cup fresh rosemary, chopped
- ¼ cup fresh thyme, chopped
- 3 Tbsp olive oil
- Salt and pepper to taste

Directions:

1. Preheat oven to 375°F (190°C)
2. In a bowl, mix together olive oil, lemon juice, minced garlic, rosemary, thyme, salt, and pepper to create a marinade
3. Rub the marinade inside and out of each game hen
4. Place lemon wedges inside the cavity of the hens
5. Roast in the oven for 1 hr. or until the juices run clear and the skin is golden brown

Tips:

- Allow the hens to rest for 10 min. before serving to keep the juices locked in
- Can be served with a side of steamed green beans or roasted sweet potatoes for a complete meal
- Save the roasted lemon as a garnish for extra flavor and presentation

Nutritional Values: Calories: 410, Fat: 28g, Carbs: 8g, Protein: 32g, Sugar: 2g, Sodium: 80 mg, Potassium: 500 mg, Cholesterol: 150 mg

DIJON MUSTARD ZESTY CHICKEN DRUMSTICKS

Preparation Time: 10 min.
Cooking Time: 45 min.
Mode of Cooking: Baking
Servings: 6
Ingredients:

- 12 chicken drumsticks
- ¼ cup Dijon mustard
- 1 Tbsp apple cider vinegar
- 1 Tbsp olive oil
- 1 tsp garlic powder
- 1 tsp onion powder
- 1 tsp dried thyme
- Salt and pepper to taste
- Fresh parsley, chopped for garnish

Directions:

1. Preheat oven to 375°F (190°C)
2. In a bowl, mix together Dijon mustard, apple cider vinegar, olive oil, garlic powder, onion powder, thyme, salt, and pepper to create a marinade
3. Coat each drumstick evenly with the marinade and arrange on a baking sheet
4. Bake in the oven for 45 min. or until the drumsticks are fully cooked and have a crispy skin

Tips:

- Serve hot and garnish with fresh parsley
- Pair this dish with a tangy coleslaw or a fresh cucumber salad for a refreshing contrast
- Leftovers can be used to make a hearty chicken salad the next day

Nutritional Values: Calories: 335, Fat: 19g, Carbs: 4g, Protein: 35g, Sugar: 1g, Sodium: 200 mg, Potassium: 340 mg, Cholesterol: 180 mg

CITRUS-HERB ROASTED CHICKEN

Preparation Time: 15 min.
Cooking Time: 1 hr. 20 min.
Mode of Cooking: Roasting
Servings: 4
Ingredients:

- 1 whole chicken approx. 5 lb.
- 1 Tbsp olive oil
- 1 tsp ground black pepper
- 1 tsp sea salt
- 2 oranges, quartered
- 1 lemon, quartered
- 4 sprigs fresh thyme
- 4 sprigs fresh rosemary
- 2 cloves garlic, minced
- 1 onion, quartered

Directions:

1. Preheat oven to 425°F (220°C)
2. Rinse chicken and pat dry with paper towels
3. Rub chicken inside and out with olive oil, black pepper, and sea salt
4. Stuff cavity with orange, lemon, thyme, rosemary, garlic, and onion pieces
5. Place chicken on roasting rack and roast in the oven until juices run clear, or an internal temperature reaches 165°F (74°C), about 80 min.

Tips:

- Before roasting, let the chicken sit at room temperature for 30 min. to ensure even cooking
- Save the pan juices to make a delicious sauce
- Incorporate the citrus skins into compost for an environmentally friendly tip

Nutritional Values: Calories: 410, Fat: 30g, Carbs: 5g, Protein: 35g, Sugar: 3g, Sodium: 390mg, Potassium: 370mg, Cholesterol: 130mg

SPICY TURMERIC CHICKEN KEBABS

Preparation Time: 25 min.
Cooking Time: 15 min.
Mode of Cooking: Grilling
Servings: 6
Ingredients:

- 2 lb. skinless boneless chicken breasts, cubed
- 2 Tbsp olive oil
- 1 Tbsp ground turmeric
- 1 tsp cayenne pepper
- 2 tsp sea salt
- 1 tsp black pepper
- Juice of 1 lime
- 1 red onion, quartered and layers separated
- Lime wedges for serving

Directions:
1. Preheat grill to medium-high heat (around 375°F or 190°C)
2. In a bowl, mix olive oil, turmeric, cayenne pepper, sea salt, black pepper, and lime juice
3. Toss chicken cubes in the marinade until well coated
4. Thread chicken and red onion layers alternately on skewers
5. Grill kebabs, turning occasionally until chicken is golden and cooked through, about 15 min.

Tips:
- Marinate chicken for at least 2 hr. before grilling for enhanced flavor
- Serve with fresh lime wedges to boost flavor
- Use bamboo skewers soaked in water to prevent burning during grilling

Nutritional Values: Calories: 280, Fat: 10g, Carbs: 4g, Protein: 43g, Sugar: 1g, Sodium: 720mg, Potassium: 300mg, Cholesterol: 120mg

CHAPTER 10: SEAFOOD AND FISH RECIPES

Welcome to the delightful realm of seafood and fish, where the bounty of the ocean meets your kitchen with endless possibilities for nourishment and enjoyment. The benefits of incorporating fish into your diet are vast, ranging from heart health to mental clarity, and it's all thanks to the high levels of omega-3 fatty acids found especially in fatty fish like salmon, mackerel, and sardines. But the advantages don't stop there—seafood is a formidable ally in maintaining a robust immune system, glowing skin, and an overall optimized health profile.

For those venturing through the Whole30 journey, the ocean's harvest offers a refreshing diversity from land-based protein sources. It's easy to fall into the routine of poultry and meat; however, the inclusion of fish and seafood can enliven your meals, bringing not only nutritional wealth but also culinary excitement. Each recipe in this chapter showcases the ease and simplicity with which these dishes can be prepared—all aligning with the Whole30 guidelines to support you and your family's health endeavors.

Imagine starting your day with a zestful shrimp skillet or winding down with a hearty, nourishing salmon stew that warms the soul. Whether you are seeking a quick weeknight fix like a seared tuna salad or planning a special weekend family meal with a whole baked fish centerpiece, these recipes are designed to cater to varied palates and schedules. Moreover, they repel the monotony that often shadows lengthy diet plans, ensuring that each meal not only sustains but excites.

Embrace this chapter as your guide to exploring the nutritional powerhouse that is seafood. With combinations ranging from the traditional to the exotic, each dish promises not just to satisfy your dietary requirements but also to inspire a lasting love for the flavors of the ocean. Dive deep into these waters, and let the variety and simplicity of these meals make a splash in your Whole30 adventure, proving that healthy eating does not have to be mundane but a celebration of natural, whole foods.

CITRUS-INFUSED GRILLED HALIBUT

Preparation Time: 15 min.
Cooking Time: 10 min.
Mode of Cooking: Grilling
Servings: 4
Ingredients:

- 4 halibut fillets (6 oz. each)
- 2 Tbsp olive oil
- 1 large orange, zested and juiced
- 1 large lemon, zested and juiced
- 2 cloves garlic, minced
- 1 tsp fresh thyme, finely chopped
- Salt and pepper to taste

Directions:

1. Preheat grill to medium-high heat
2. In a small bowl, combine olive oil, orange juice and zest, lemon juice and zest, garlic, thyme, salt, and pepper
3. Brush halibut fillets with citrus marinade
4. Place fillets on grill; grill each side for about 5 minutes or until fish flakes easily with a fork

Tips:

- Use remaining marinade to baste the fillets while grilling for extra flavor
- Serve with a side of grilled asparagus for a complete meal

- Citrus fruits like orange and lemon not only add flavor but also help in marinating the fish quickly, making it a great choice for a quick meal

Nutritional Values: Calories: 240, Fat: 10g, Carbs: 3g, Protein: 34g, Sugar: 1g, Sodium: 70 mg, Potassium: 840 mg, Cholesterol: 45 mg

---

SPICY SHRIMP AND CAULIFLOWER GRITS

Preparation Time: 20 min.
Cooking Time: 15 min.
Mode of Cooking: Sautéing
Servings: 4
Ingredients:

- 24 large shrimp, peeled and deveined
- 4 cups cauliflower, riced
- 1 cup coconut milk
- 2 Tbsp ghee
- 1 tsp smoked paprika
- 1/2 tsp cayenne pepper
- Salt to taste
- Fresh parsley, chopped for garnish

Directions:

1. In a large skillet, heat ghee over medium heat
2. Add riced cauliflower and sauté until soft, about 8 minutes
3. Stir in coconut milk and simmer until thickened, about 7 minutes
4. Season with salt
5. In another skillet, combine shrimp with smoked paprika, cayenne pepper, and salt
6. Sauté shrimp until pink and cooked through, about 5-7 minutes
7. Serve shrimp over cauliflower grits and garnish with fresh parsley

Tips:

- For a less spicy version, reduce the amount of cayenne pepper
- Shrimp can be substituted with chicken or fish for variety
- To enhance flavor, add a squeeze of lemon juice over the shrimp when serving

Nutritional Values: Calories: 330, Fat: 20g, Carbs: 12g, Protein: 25g, Sugar: 5g, Sodium: 300 mg, Potassium: 700 mg, Cholesterol: 180 mg

---

LEMON DILL SALMON SKEWERS

Preparation Time: 25 min.
Cooking Time: 10 min.
Mode of Cooking: Grilling
Servings: 4
Ingredients:

- 4 salmon fillets (5 oz. each), cut into chunks
- 2 Tbsp olive oil
- 1 Tbsp fresh dill, finely chopped

- 2 Tbsp lemon juice
- 1 lemon, sliced into thin rounds
- Salt and pepper to taste

Directions:

1. Preheat grill to medium heat
2. In a bowl, whisk together olive oil, lemon juice, chopped dill, salt, and pepper
3. Thread salmon chunks and lemon slices alternately onto skewers
4. Grill skewers for about 5 minutes on each side or until salmon is cooked through and opaque

Tips:

- Serve these skewers with a side of mixed greens for a fresh, balanced meal
- Soaking the skewers in water for 30 minutes before grilling can prevent them from burning
- Dill and lemon pair perfectly with salmon, enhancing its flavor without overpowering it

Nutritional Values: Calories: 280, Fat: 15g, Carbs: 3g, Protein: 31g, Sugar: 1g, Sodium: 75 mg, Potassium: 830 mg, Cholesterol: 85 mg

MEDITERRANEAN TUNA STEAKS

Preparation Time: 10 min.
Cooking Time: 12 min.
Mode of Cooking: Broiling
Servings: 4
Ingredients:

- 4 tuna steaks (6 oz. each)
- 2 Tbsp olive oil
- 1 tsp rosemary, finely chopped
- 1 tsp thyme, finely chopped
- 2 cloves garlic, minced
- 1/2 cup Kalamata olives, pitted and chopped
- 1/2 cup sundried tomatoes, chopped
- Salt and pepper to taste

Directions:

1. Preheat broiler and grease a broiling pan
2. In a small bowl, combine olive oil, rosemary, thyme, garlic, salt, and pepper
3. Brush mixture over tuna steaks
4. Broil for 6 minutes per side or until desired doneness is achieved
5. Top each steak with chopped olives and sundried tomatoes before serving

Tips:

- Garnish with fresh basil for an extra touch of Mediterranean flavor
- Pair with a simple arugula salad dressed with olive oil and lemon juice for a complete meal
- Adjust cooking time based on thickness of the tuna steaks for perfect doneness

Nutritional Values: Calories: 310, Fat: 14g, Carbs: 9g, Protein: 38g, Sugar: 4g, Sodium: 480 mg, Potassium: 770 mg, Cholesterol: 60 mg

SCALLOP AND VEGETABLE STIR-FRY

Preparation Time: 15 min.
Cooking Time: 15 min.
Mode of Cooking: Stir-Frying
Servings: 4
Ingredients:

- 12 large scallops
- 2 cups broccoli florets
- 1 red bell pepper, sliced
- 1 yellow bell pepper, sliced
- 1 cup snap peas
- 2 Tbsp coconut oil
- 2 Tbsp ginger, minced
- 3 Tbsp coconut aminos
- Salt and pepper to taste

Directions:

1. Heat coconut oil in a large skillet over medium-high heat
2. Add ginger and sauté for 1 minute
3. Add scallops and cook for 2 minutes on each side or until opaque
4. Remove scallops from skillet
5. Add broccoli, bell peppers, and snap peas to the skillet; stir-fry for about 7 minutes or until vegetables are tender-crisp
6. Return scallops to skillet, add coconut aminos, and toss to combine

Tips:

- Opt for fresh scallops for better texture and flavor
- Coconut aminos provide a sweet-salty flavor that complements the scallops well
- Serve with cauliflower rice to keep it Whole30 compliant

Nutritional Values: Calories: 220, Fat: 10g, Carbs: 14g, Protein: 19g, Sugar: 6g, Sodium: 400 mg, Potassium: 460 mg, Cholesterol: 35 mg

LEMON-THYME ROASTED SNAPPER

Preparation Time: 15 min
Cooking Time: 40 min
Mode of Cooking: Roasting
Servings: 4
Ingredients:

- 2 lb. whole snapper, cleaned and scaled
- 4 slices fresh lemon
- 2 sprigs fresh thyme
- 3 Tbsp extra virgin olive oil
- 1 tsp sea salt
- 1/2 tsp cracked black pepper

- 1 lemon, zested and squeezed

Directions:

1. Preheat oven to 400°F (204°C)
2. Rinse snapper and pat dry
3. Place lemon slices and thyme inside the cavity of the snapper
4. Rub the outside of the fish with olive oil, lemon zest, and juice
5. Season with salt and pepper
6. Roast in the oven until the flesh flakes easily, about 40 min

Tips:

- Remember to check the internal temperature reaches 145°F (63°C) for safety
- Serve with a fresh green salad to complement the flavors

Nutritional Values: Calories: 240, Fat: 10g, Carbs: 1g, Protein: 35g, Sugar: 0g, Sodium: 620 mg, Potassium: 560 mg, Cholesterol: 60 mg

---

SPICY COCONUT SHRIMP STEW

Preparation Time: 20 min
Cooking Time: 25 min
Mode of Cooking: Simmering
Servings: 6
Ingredients:

- 1 lb. shrimp, peeled and deveined
- 1 can (14 oz.) coconut milk
- 2 cups diced tomatoes
- 1 cup vegetable broth
- 1 onion, thinly sliced
- 3 cloves garlic, minced
- 2 Tbsp coconut oil
- 1 Tbsp curry powder
- 1/2 tsp red pepper flakes
- Fresh cilantro for garnish
- Salt to taste

Directions:

1. Heat coconut oil in a large pot over medium heat
2. Sauté onion and garlic until translucent
3. Add curry powder and red pepper flakes, cook for 1 min
4. Pour in coconut milk, vegetable broth, and tomatoes
5. Bring to a simmer and add shrimp
6. Cook until shrimp is opaque and cooked through, about 15 min

Tips:

- Garnish with fresh cilantro before serving
- Adjust the level of spiciness by increasing or decreasing red pepper flakes as desired

Nutritional Values: Calories: 215, Fat: 15g, Carbs: 8g, Protein: 15g, Sugar: 2g, Sodium: 300 mg, Potassium: 300 mg, Cholesterol: 120 mg

HERBED HALIBUT PACKETS

Preparation Time: 10 min
Cooking Time: 20 min
Mode of Cooking: Baking
Servings: 4
Ingredients:

- 4 halibut fillets, about 6 oz each
- 2 zucchinis, thinly sliced
- 1 bell pepper, julienned
- 2 Tbsp chopped fresh dill
- 2 Tbsp chopped fresh parsley
- 4 tsp extra virgin olive oil
- Salt and pepper to taste
- Lemon wedges, for serving

Directions:

1. Preheat oven to 375°F (190°C)
2. Cut four sheets of foil
3. Place one halibut fillet on each sheet, top with zucchini and bell pepper
4. Sprinkle with dill, parsley, salt, and pepper
5. Drizzle with olive oil
6. Fold the foil around the fish to create a packet, sealing the edges tightly
7. Bake until fish is cooked through, about 20 min

Tips:

- Serve immediately with lemon wedges for extra zest
- Cooking in foil packets helps to retain moisture and flavors

Nutritional Values: Calories: 220, Fat: 9g, Carbs: 4g, Protein: 30g, Sugar: 2g, Sodium: 300 mg, Potassium: 800 mg, Cholesterol: 45 mg

CITRUS GINGER TUNA STEAKS

Preparation Time: 10 min
Cooking Time: 10 min
Mode of Cooking: Grilling
Servings: 4
Ingredients:

- 4 tuna steaks, about 6 oz each
- 1/4 cup fresh orange juice
- 1 Tbsp grated ginger
- 2 Tbsp soy sauce (compliant with Whole30)
- 1 Tbsp olive oil
- 1 Tbsp lime juice

- 1 tsp crushed garlic
- Black pepper to taste

Directions:

1. Preheat grill to medium-high heat
2. Whisk together orange juice, ginger, soy sauce, olive oil, lime juice, and garlic in a bowl
3. Season tuna steaks with black pepper and marinate in the mixture for 10 min
4. Grill steaks until desired doneness, about 5 min per side for medium rare

Tips:

- Marinating the tuna adds depth and zest to the flavor
- Do not overcook to maintain the tenderness of the fish

Nutritional Values: Calories: 200, Fat: 5g, Carbs: 3g, Protein: 35g, Sugar: 1g, Sodium: 330 mg, Potassium: 500 mg, Cholesterol: 50 mg

SAFFRON INFUSED MUSSELS

Preparation Time: 15 min
Cooking Time: 10 min
Mode of Cooking: Steaming
Servings: 4
Ingredients:

- 2 lbs mussels, cleaned and debearded
- 1 cup white wine
- 2 Tbsp ghee
- 1 large onion, finely chopped
- 1 tsp saffron threads
- 3 cloves garlic, minced
- Fresh parsley, chopped for garnish
- Lemon wedges, for serving

Directions:

1. Heat ghee in a large pot over medium heat
2. Add onion and garlic, sauté until soft
3. Add saffron and stir for 1 min
4. Pour in white wine and bring to a boil
5. Add mussels and cover the pot
6. Steam until all mussels are opened, about 10 min

Tips:

- Discard any mussels that do not open
- Serve hot, garnished with chopped parsley and lemon wedges on the side

Nutritional Values: Calories: 180, Fat: 8g, Carbs: 10g, Protein: 18g, Sugar: 0g, Sodium: 290 mg, Potassium: 350 mg, Cholesterol: 50 mg

LEMON HERB BAKED COD

Preparation Time: 10 min
Cooking Time: 20 min
Mode of Cooking: Baking
Servings: 4
Ingredients:

- 4 (6 oz) cod filets
- 2 Tbsp extra virgin olive oil
- 1 lemon, zested and juiced
- 3 garlic cloves, finely minced
- 1 Tbsp fresh thyme, chopped
- 1 Tbsp fresh parsley, chopped
- Salt and freshly ground black pepper to taste

Directions:

1. Preheat oven to 400°F (200°C)
2. In a small bowl, combine olive oil, lemon zest, lemon juice, garlic, thyme, and parsley to form a marinade
3. Season the cod filets with salt and pepper and lay them in a baking dish
4. Pour the marinade over the cod and ensure each filet is evenly coated
5. Bake in the preheated oven for 20 min or until cod flakes easily with a fork

Tips:

- Marinate the cod for at least 20 minutes before baking for enhanced flavor
- Serve with a side of steamed green vegetables for a complete meal

Nutritional Values: Calories: 190, Fat: 7g, Carbs: 1g, Protein: 30g, Sugar: 0g, Sodium: 70 mg, Potassium: 460 mg, Cholesterol: 60 mg

SPICY SHRIMP SKILLET

Preparation Time: 15 min
Cooking Time: 10 min
Mode of Cooking: Sautéing
Servings: 4
Ingredients:

- 1 lb large shrimp, peeled and deveined
- 2 Tbsp coconut oil
- 1 red bell pepper, sliced
- 1 yellow bell pepper, sliced
- 2 tsp smoked paprika
- 1 tsp ground cumin
- ½ tsp crushed red pepper flakes
- 2 Tbsp cilantro, chopped
- Salt and freshly ground black pepper to taste

Directions:

1. Heat coconut oil in a large skillet over medium-high heat

2. Add the bell peppers and sauté for 5 min until they begin to soften
3. Add the shrimp, smoked paprika, cumin, and red pepper flakes
4. Cook for 5 min or until the shrimp are pink and cooked through
5. Season with salt and pepper and garnish with chopped cilantro before serving

Tips:

- Serve over cauliflower rice for a Whole30 compliant meal
- Adjust the level of spice to suit your taste preferences

Nutritional Values: Calories: 240, Fat: 12g, Carbs: 6g, Protein: 26g, Sugar: 2g, Sodium: 200 mg, Potassium: 300 mg, Cholesterol: 185 mg

CHAPTER 11: WHOLESOME SAUCES AND DRESSINGS

In the vibrant world of Whole30, where each meal is an opportunity to nourish and rejuvenate, the power of a good sauce or dressing can be a game changer. Imagine transforming a simple grilled chicken or a vibrant bowl of mixed greens into a culinary delight with just a drizzle of the right condiment. That's the magic we're diving into in this chapter.

Sauces and dressings are more than mere additions; they are the secret heroes of the culinary world, bringing together diverse flavors and turning wholesome ingredients into exciting dishes. Whole30 emphasizes eating foods in their whole, unprocessed form, and this philosophy extends to the sauces and dressings we use. Here, you'll learn to craft them from scratch, using natural ingredients that align with the Whole30 principles.

Crafting your sauces and dressings means you have control over what goes into your body—no hidden sugars, no preservatives, just pure, wholesome goodness. Whether it's a creamy avocado dressing to add a touch of luxury to your salads, or a spicy homemade salsa to give a kick to your taco nights, the recipes you will find here are designed to be easy, quick, and above all, healthful.

What makes these condiments truly stand out is their versatility. A good dressing can double as a marinade, a vibrant sauce can be the basis of a stir-fry, and a dab of homemade pesto can transform a mundane dish into a taste sensation. This adaptability makes them invaluable tools in your Whole30 toolkit, helping you to maintain variety in your diet and keep mealtime exciting and satisfying.

Throughout this chapter, we'll explore a variety of sauces and dressings, each crafted to compliment your journey towards better health without sacrificing flavor. Prepare to unlock the secrets to zesty vinaigrettes, robust tomato sauces, and more—each a tiny titan of taste that promises to keep your palate delighted and your body nourished.

AVOCADO CILANTRO LIME DRESSING

Preparation Time: 10 min.
Cooking Time: none
Mode of Cooking: No Cooking
Servings: 8
Ingredients:

- 1 ripe avocado, peeled and pitted
- 1/4 cup fresh lime juice
- 1/3 cup cilantro leaves, lightly packed
- 1 clove garlic, minced
- 1/2 tsp ground cumin
- 1/4 cup olive oil
- Salt and freshly ground black pepper to taste
- 1/3 cup water to thin, as needed

Directions:

1. Combine avocado, lime juice, cilantro, garlic, cumin, and olive oil in a blender
2. Blend until smooth, adding water slowly to reach desired consistency
3. Season with salt and pepper to taste

Tips:

- Consider adding a touch of fresh chili for a spicy kick
- If dressing thickens when stored, thin with a little water before serving

Nutritional Values: Calories: 110, Fat: 10g, Carbs: 6g, Protein: 1g, Sugar: 0g, Sodium: 20 mg, Potassium: 200 mg, Cholesterol: 0 mg

ROASTED GARLIC AND LEMON VINAIGRETTE

Preparation Time: 15 min.
Cooking Time: 45 min.
Mode of Cooking: Roasting
Servings: 6
Ingredients:

- 1 head garlic
- 2 Tbsp olive oil for roasting
- 1/4 cup fresh lemon juice
- 1/2 tsp Dijon mustard (check for compliance with Whole30)
- 1/2 cup extra virgin olive oil
- Sea salt to taste
- Freshly cracked black pepper to taste

Directions:

1. Preheat oven to 400°F (200°C)
2. Cut the top off the head of garlic, drizzle with olive oil and wrap in foil
3. Roast in the oven for 45 min. or until cloves are soft and caramelized
4. Squeeze the roasted garlic into a blender, add lemon juice, Dijon mustard, and blend until smooth
5. Slowly incorporate the extra virgin olive oil to emulsify, season with salt and pepper

Tips:

- Roasted garlic can be made in advance and stored in the refrigerator
- Use organic lemons for the best flavor

Nutritional Values: Calories: 170, Fat: 18g, Carbs: 2g, Protein: 0g, Sugar: 0g, Sodium: 30 mg, Potassium: 10 mg, Cholesterol: 0 mg

SPICY TOMATO TAHINI SAUCE

Preparation Time: 10 min.
Cooking Time: none
Mode of Cooking: No Cooking
Servings: 4
Ingredients:

- 1/2 cup tahini
- 1/4 cup water
- 1 Tbsp apple cider vinegar
- 1/2 cup tomato paste
- 1 tsp smoked paprika
- Sea salt to taste
- 1/2 tsp cayenne pepper (or to taste)

Directions:

1. Mix tahini, water, and apple cider vinegar in a mixing bowl until smooth

2. Stir in tomato paste, smoked paprika, sea salt, and cayenne pepper until well combined
3. Adjust seasoning and water for consistency as needed

Tips:

- Great as a dressing or dip for veggies
- Adjust cayenne pepper according to heat preference
- Can be stored in the refrigerator for up to a week

Nutritional Values: Calories: 140, Fat: 12g, Carbs: 8g, Protein: 4g, Sugar: 3g, Sodium: 60 mg, Potassium: 210 mg, Cholesterol: 0 mg

CREAMY HERB DRESSING (DAIRY-FREE)

Preparation Time: 15 min.
Cooking Time: none
Mode of Cooking: No Cooking
Servings: 8
Ingredients:

- 1/2 cup coconut cream
- 1/4 cup chives, finely chopped
- 1/4 cup parsley, finely chopped
- 1 Tbsp lemon juice
- Salt and freshly ground black pepper to taste
- 1 clove garlic, minced

Directions:

1. Combine coconut cream, chives, parsley, lemon juice, and minced garlic in a bowl
2. Whisk thoroughly until well combined and creamy
3. Season with salt and pepper to taste

Tips:

- Serve over fresh salads or grilled vegetables
- If dressing is too thick, thin with a little bit of water or additional lemon juice
- Keep refrigerated and use within 5 days

Nutritional Values: Calories: 80, Fat: 8g, Carbs: 2g, Protein: 1g, Sugar: 0g, Sodium: 5 mg, Potassium: 25 mg, Cholesterol: 0 mg

MINT AND AVOCADO GREEN GODDESS DRESSING

Preparation Time: 8 min.
Cooking Time: none
Mode of Cooking: No Cooking
Servings: 5
Ingredients:

- 1 ripe avocado
- 1/4 cup fresh mint leaves
- 1/4 cup fresh basil leaves
- 1/4 cup chives
- 1/4 cup lemon juice

- 1/4 cup olive oil
- Salt and freshly ground black pepper to taste
- Water as needed to thin

Directions:

1. Blend avocado, mint, basil, chives, lemon juice, and olive oil in a food processor until smooth
2. Season with salt and black pepper to taste
3. Add water gradually until desired consistency is achieved

Tips:

- Perfect for drizzling over grilled chicken or fish
- Refreshing addition to summer salads
- Can be stored in an airtight container in the refrigerator for up to 3 days

Nutritional Values: Calories: 120, Fat: 11g, Carbs: 4g, Protein: 1g, Sugar: 0g, Sodium: 10 mg, Potassium: 150 mg, Cholesterol: 0 mg

CITRUS GINGER DRESSING

Preparation Time: 5 min
Cooking Time: none
Mode of Cooking: No Cooking
Servings: 4
Ingredients:

- Juice of 1 orange
- Juice of 1 lemon
- 1 Tbsp fresh ginger, grated
- 2 Tbsp extra virgin olive oil
- 1 tsp apple cider vinegar
- 1 clove garlic, minced
- 1 Tbsp fresh cilantro, finely chopped
- Salt and pepper to taste

Directions:

1. Combine orange juice, lemon juice, grated ginger, olive oil, apple cider vinegar, minced garlic, and chopped cilantro in a mixing bowl
2. Whisk thoroughly until all ingredients are well blended
3. Season with salt and pepper to taste

Tips:

- Store in a glass jar in the refrigerator for enhanced flavor development
- Shake well before each use to re-emulsify

Nutritional Values: Calories: 60, Fat: 5g, Carbs: 4g, Protein: 0g, Sugar: 2g, Sodium: 5 mg, Potassium: 20 mg, Cholesterol: 0 mg

CILANTRO LIME DRESSING

Preparation Time: 10 min.
Cooking Time: none
Mode of Cooking: No Cooking

Servings: 8

Ingredients:

- 1 cup fresh cilantro, stems removed
- juice of 2 limes
- 1/3 cup extra virgin olive oil
- 1 clove garlic, minced
- 1 Tbsp apple cider vinegar
- salt and pepper to taste
- 1/2 tsp ground cumin

Directions:

1. Combine cilantro, lime juice, olive oil, minced garlic, and apple cider vinegar in a blender
2. Blend until smooth
3. Season with salt, pepper, and cumin
4. Adjust flavors according to taste

Tips:

- Refrigerate dressing to enhance flavors before serving
- Can be used as a marinade for chicken or fish for a zesty twist
- Blend with avocado for a creamy variation

Nutritional Values: Calories: 80, Fat: 9g, Carbs: 1g, Protein: 0g, Sugar: 0g, Sodium: 2 mg, Potassium: 20 mg, Cholesterol: 0 mg

SMOKY TOMATO VINAIGRETTE

Preparation Time: 15 min.

Cooking Time: none

Mode of Cooking: No Cooking

Servings: 6

Ingredients:

- 1/2 cup sun-dried tomatoes, not oil-packed
- 3/4 cup boiling water
- 1/4 cup red wine vinegar
- 1 clove garlic, minced
- 1 tsp smoked paprika
- 1/2 tsp Dijon mustard
- 1/2 cup olive oil
- salt and black pepper to taste

Directions:

1. Soak sun-dried tomatoes in boiling water for 10 min. to rehydrate
2. Drain and place tomatoes in blender with red wine vinegar, garlic, smoked paprika, and Dijon mustard
3. Blend until combined
4. Gradually add olive oil while blending until emulsified
5. Season with salt and pepper

Tips:

- Serve over grilled vegetables for an extra layer of flavor
- Store in airtight container in the refrigerator
- Shake well before using as natural separation may occur

Nutritional Values: Calories: 90, Fat: 10g, Carbs: 2g, Protein: 0g, Sugar: 1g, Sodium: 55 mg, Potassium: 30 mg, Cholesterol: 0 mg

CREAMY AVOCADO HERB DRESSING

Preparation Time: 10 min.
Cooking Time: none
Mode of Cooking: No Cooking
Servings: 8
Ingredients:

- 2 ripe avocados
- 1/2 cup coconut milk (full-fat)
- juice of 1 lemon
- 1/4 cup fresh parsley, chopped
- 1 Tbsp chives, chopped
- 1 clove garlic
- salt and pepper to taste

Directions:

1. Scoop the avocado flesh into a blender
2. Add coconut milk, lemon juice, parsley, chives, and garlic
3. Blend until smooth and creamy
4. Season with salt and pepper to taste

Tips:

- Use immediately or store in refrigerator
- Perfect for drizzling over a fresh salad or as a dip for crudités
- If the dressing thickens in the fridge, whisk in a few tablespoons of water to thin before serving

Nutritional Values: Calories: 130, Fat: 12g, Carbs: 6g, Protein: 1g, Sugar: 1g, Sodium: 10 mg, Potassium: 200 mg, Cholesterol: 0 mg

SPICED GINGER-SESAME DRESSING

Preparation Time: 10 min.
Cooking Time: none
Mode of Cooking: No Cooking
Servings: 8
Ingredients:

- 1/4 cup sesame oil
- 1/4 cup coconut aminos
- 2 Tbsp fresh ginger, grated
- 1 Tbsp apple cider vinegar
- 1 Tbsp sesame seeds

- 1/2 tsp red pepper flakes

Directions:

1. Combine sesame oil, coconut aminos, grated ginger, apple cider vinegar, sesame seeds, and red pepper flakes in a jar
2. Screw the lid on tightly and shake until all ingredients are well mixed

Tips:

- Store in the refrigerator for up to 1 week
- Great for an Asian-inspired salad or as a drizzle over steamed vegetables
- Ginger can be adjusted for more or less heat

Nutritional Values: Calories: 70, Fat: 7g, Carbs: 1g, Protein: 1g, Sugar: 0g, Sodium: 150 mg, Potassium: 30 mg, Cholesterol: 0 mg

---

LEMON TAHINI DRESSING

Preparation Time: 10 min.
Cooking Time: none
Mode of Cooking: No Cooking
Servings: 6
Ingredients:

- 1/3 cup tahini
- juice of 2 lemons
- 2 cloves garlic, minced
- 1 Tbsp olive oil
- 1/4 tsp sea salt
- water to thin (approximately 1/4 cup)

Directions:

1. In a bowl, whisk together tahini, lemon juice, minced garlic, olive oil, and sea salt
2. Gradually add water while whisking until desired consistency is reached

Tips:

- Ideal for drizzling over roasted vegetables or as a healthy dressing for bowls
- The dressing can be thickened or thinned by adjusting the amount of water added
- Enhance the flavor by adding fresh herbs

Nutritional Values: Calories: 130, Fat: 12g, Carbs: 3g, Protein: 2g, Sugar: 0g, Sodium: 60 mg, Potassium: 50 mg, Cholesterol: 0 mg

---

CITRUS AVOCADO DRESSING

Preparation Time: 10 min.
Cooking Time: none
Mode of Cooking: No Cooking
Servings: 4
Ingredients:

- 1 ripe avocado, peeled and pitted
- Juice of 1 orange
- Juice of 1 lime
- 1 Tbsp olive oil

- 1 clove garlic, minced
- 1 tsp fresh ginger, grated
- Salt and freshly ground black pepper to taste
- ¼ cup cilantro, finely chopped

Directions:

1. Combine avocado, orange juice, lime juice, olive oil, garlic, and ginger in a blender and blend until smooth
2. Season with salt and pepper to taste
3. Stir in cilantro just before serving

Tips:

- Try adding a pinch of cayenne for a spicy kick
- Use as a dressing over fresh greens or as a creamy sauce for grilled chicken

Nutritional Values: Calories: 120, Fat: 10g, Carbs: 8g, Protein: 2g, Sugar: 2g, Sodium: 10 mg, Potassium: 250 mg, Cholesterol: 0 mg

CHAPTER 12: REFRESHING AND HEALTHY DRINKS

As we journey through our 30-day venture with the Whole30 program, the vitality and refreshing burst that a well-crafted drink can bring to our day should not be underestimated. In a world where our palates are often dulled by overly sweetened and artificially flavored beverages, this chapter invites you to rediscover the simple joy of drinks that are not only healthy but vibrantly refreshing.

Think of a drink as more than just a thirst quencher. Each sip can be a rejuvenating elixir that enhances our Whole30 experience. The drinks featured in this chapter are designed with your energy and well-being in mind, ensuring they align perfectly with the nutritional ethos of Whole30—encouraging whole, unprocessed ingredients that refresh and revitalize your body from the inside out.

Embarking on the Whole30 path has taught us the importance of mindful eating. Similarly, drinking should also be an act of nourishment. Imagine starting your day with a smoothie that's a medley of fresh fruits, greens, and seeds—each ingredient selected to energize your mornings without the crash that comes from high-sugar options. Or picture winding down your day with a soothing herbal tea that not only calms your mind but also supports your digestive health.

In this chapter, we move away from conventional drink choices and explore a variety of recipes from invigorating morning blends to soothing evening sips that promise to keep your hydration as exciting and varied as the foods on your plate. Through a kaleidoscope of flavors—from the zing of citrus to the gentle sweetness of berries, enhanced by herbs and spices—these drinks are crafted to complement your meals and support your health journey, ensuring your hydration is anything but mundane.

As we continue, let each recipe serve as an inspiration for you to take these foundational ideas, adapt them with seasonal fruits or personal taste preferences, and make them a beloved part of your Whole30 adventure. The power of a good drink lies not just in its nutritional value, but in its ability to elevate the moment, nourish the body, and delight the senses. Cheers to enriching our days with simplicity and vitality!

CUCUMBER MINT REFRESH

Preparation Time: 5 min.
Cooking Time: none
Mode of Cooking: No Cooking
Servings: 2
Ingredients:

- 1 large cucumber, peeled and chopped
- 10 fresh mint leaves
- Juice of 2 limes
- 1 Tbsp honey (omit for strict Whole30, optional for taste-adjusting post-Whole30)
- 2 cups ice water
- Extra mint leaves and lime slices for garnish

Directions:

1. Blend cucumber, mint leaves, lime juice, and honey (if using) in a blender until smooth
2. Strain the mixture through a fine mesh sieve into a pitcher
3. Stir in ice water until well combined
4. Serve chilled, garnished with mint leaves and lime slices

Tips:
- Add sparkling water instead of still water for a fizzy alternative
- If you find the drink too tart, adjust the sweetness by adding a bit more honey if not on strict Whole30

Nutritional Values: Calories: 72, Fat: 0.2g, Carbs: 18g, Protein: 1g, Sugar: 12g, Sodium: 3 mg, Potassium: 287 mg, Cholesterol: 0 mg

SPICY PINEAPPLE ZINGER

Preparation Time: 10 min.
Cooking Time: none
Mode of Cooking: No Cooking
Servings: 4
Ingredients:
- 2 cups fresh pineapple chunks
- 1 small red chili, deseeded and minced
- Juice of 1 orange
- 1 Tbsp freshly grated ginger
- 4 cups cold water
- Ice cubes
- Fresh pineapple slices for garnish

Directions:
1. Blend pineapple chunks, red chili, orange juice, and grated ginger together until smooth
2. Pour over a sieve into a large jug to remove pulp and seeds
3. Add cold water and stir well
4. Serve over ice, garnished with pineapple slices

Tips:
- Use gloves when handling chili to avoid skin irritation
- For a milder drink, remove all seeds from the chili before usage
- Serve immediately for best flavor and zing

Nutritional Values: Calories: 76, Fat: 0.5g, Carbs: 19g, Protein: 1g, Sugar: 14g, Sodium: 5 mg, Potassium: 195 mg, Cholesterol: 0 mg

GOLDEN TURMERIC TEA

Preparation Time: 8 min.
Cooking Time: none
Mode of Cooking: No Cooking
Servings: 2
Ingredients:
- 2 cups coconut milk
- 1 tsp turmeric powder
- 1/2 tsp cinnamon
- 1/4 tsp black pepper
- 1 Tbsp coconut oil
- 1 Tbsp honey (omit for strict Whole30, optional for post-Whole30)

- Cinnamon sticks for garnish

Directions:

1. Warm coconut milk in a saucepan over medium heat but do not boil
2. Whisk in turmeric powder, cinnamon, and black pepper until well combined
3. Remove from heat and stir in coconut oil and honey if using
4. Pour into cups and garnish with cinnamon sticks

Tips:

- Serve warm for a comforting evening drink
- If too strong, adjust turmeric and cinnamon to taste
- Stir well before drinking, as spices tend to settle

Nutritional Values: Calories: 161, Fat: 15g, Carbs: 6g, Protein: 1g, Sugar: 0g, Sodium: 25 mg, Potassium: 50 mg, Cholesterol: 0 mg

---

LEMON GINGER FLUSH

Preparation Time: 7 min.
Cooking Time: none
Mode of Cooking: No Cooking
Servings: 1
Ingredients:

- 1 inch fresh ginger root, peeled and sliced
- 1/2 lemon, juiced and zest finely grated
- 1 cup hot water
- 1 tsp honey (omit for strict Whole30, optional for post-Whole30)

Directions:

1. Infuse hot water with ginger slices and lemon zest for about 5 min.
2. Strain the infusion into a mug
3. Add lemon juice and honey if using, stir well to combine
4. Serve hot

Tips:

- Can be enjoyed as a morning tonic to stimulate digestion
- The infusion can be stored in a thermos and sipped throughout the day
- Increase or decrease the amount of ginger based on your preference for spiciness

Nutritional Values: Calories: 19, Fat: 0g, Carbs: 5g, Protein: 0g, Sugar: 3g, Sodium: 1 mg, Potassium: 49 mg, Cholesterol: 0 mg

---

BERRY BASIL BLAST

Preparation Time: 6 min.
Cooking Time: none
Mode of Cooking: No Cooking
Servings: 2
Ingredients:

- 1 cup fresh blueberries
- 1 cup fresh strawberries, hulled

- 6-8 fresh basil leaves
- Juice of 1 lemon
- 2 cups cold water
- Ice cubes
- Extra basil leaves and berries for garnish

Directions:

1. Blend blueberries, strawberries, basil leaves, and lemon juice until smooth
2. Strain through a fine mesh sieve to remove seeds and larger pulp
3. Mix the strained juice with cold water in a pitcher
4. Serve over ice, garnished with extra basil leaves and berries

Tips:

- Experiment with different berries for varied flavor profiles
- Basil can be replaced with mint for a cooler taste
- Perfect as a refreshing summer drink or a detox beverage

Nutritional Values: Calories: 58, Fat: 0.3g, Carbs: 14g, Protein: 1g, Sugar: 9g, Sodium: 3 mg, Potassium: 144 mg, Cholesterol: 0 mg

SPARKLING LIME AND MINT REFRESHER

Preparation Time: 5 min.
Cooking Time: none
Mode of Cooking: Mixing
Servings: 2
Ingredients:

- 1 large lime, juiced
- 10 fresh mint leaves
- 2 cups sparkling water, chilled
- 2 tsp freshly grated ginger
- Ice cubes

Directions:

1. Muddle mint leaves with lime juice and grated ginger in a pitcher
2. Add sparkling water and stir gently until well blended
3. Serve over ice in glasses

Tips:

- Use a muddler or the back of a spoon to press the mint leaves to release the oils
- For added sweetness, a dash of stevia can be incorporated
- Can be garnished with lime wheels or additional mint sprigs

Nutritional Values: Calories: 10, Fat: 0g, Carbs: 3g, Protein: 0g, Sugar: 1g, Sodium: 2 mg, Potassium: 20 mg, Cholesterol: 0 mg

CUCUMBER BASIL COOLER

Preparation Time: 3 min.
Cooking Time: none
Mode of Cooking: Blending

Servings: 2

Ingredients:

- ½ large cucumber, peeled and chopped
- 6 fresh basil leaves
- Juice of 1 lemon
- 1½ cups of ice water
- Ice cubes
- 1 tsp raw apple cider vinegar

Directions:

1. Blend cucumber, basil leaves, and lemon juice with ice water until smooth
2. Strain into glasses filled with ice
3. Stir in apple cider vinegar

Tips:

- A high-speed blender works best for a smoother consistency
- If available, sparkling water can be used to add fizz
- A pinch of salt can enhance the flavors

Nutritional Values: Calories: 8, Fat: 0.1g, Carbs: 2g, Protein: 0.4g, Sugar: 1g, Sodium: 4 mg, Potassium: 76 mg, Cholesterol: 0 mg

COCONUT GINGER ZING

Preparation Time: 7 min.
Cooking Time: none
Mode of Cooking: Mixing
Servings: 2

Ingredients:

- 1 cup coconut water
- 1 Tbsp grated fresh ginger
- Juice of ½ orange
- Juice of ½ lemon
- 1 Tbsp chia seeds
- Ice cubes

Directions:

1. Combine coconut water, grated ginger, orange juice, and lemon juice in a large shaker
2. Shake vigorously for about 1 minute
3. Pour over ice and sprinkle with chia seeds

Tips:

- Allow the mixture to sit for a few minutes after adding chia seeds to thicken slightly
- The drink can be sweetened with a small amount of crushed dates if desired
- Can be made ahead and refrigerated overnight

Nutritional Values: Calories: 70, Fat: 1.5g, Carbs: 13g, Protein: 2g, Sugar: 6g, Sodium: 40 mg, Potassium: 200 mg, Cholesterol: 0 mg

SPICY TURMERIC TONIC

Preparation Time: 6 min.
Cooking Time: none
Mode of Cooking: Stirring
Servings: 1
Ingredients:

- 1 cup warm water
- 1 tsp turmeric powder
- Juice of ½ lemon
- 1/16 tsp cayenne pepper
- 1 tsp honey (omit for Whole30, optional)
- A pinch of black pepper

Directions:

1. Stir all ingredients in a mug until well combined
2. Adjust cayenne to taste
3. Drink warm

Tips:

- Turmeric is fat-soluble, so pairing it with a fat like some coconut milk could increase absorption
- Drinking this first thing in the morning kick-starts metabolism
- Ensure to mix thoroughly to prevent turmeric from settling

Nutritional Values: Calories: 9, Fat: 0.1g, Carbs: 2.5g, Protein: 0.3g, Sugar: 0.4g, Sodium: 1 mg, Potassium: 49 mg, Cholesterol: 0 mg

HERBAL BLUEBERRY SMASH

Preparation Time: 8 min.
Cooking Time: none
Mode of Cooking: Muddling
Servings: 2
Ingredients:

- ½ cup fresh blueberries
- 2 Tbsp fresh thyme leaves
- Juice of 1 lime
- 1½ cups chilled green tea
- Ice cubes
- Optional: stevia to taste

Directions:

1. Muddle blueberries and thyme in a pitcher to release their flavors
2. Add lime juice and chilled green tea
3. Stir to combine thoroughly
4. Serve over ice in tall glasses

Tips:

- Opt for a gentle muddle to avoid turning the ingredients into a pulp
- Green tea should be brewed and cooled in advance to enhance the flavors

- Optional stevia can be added for a mild sweet touch without breaking Whole30 rules

Nutritional Values: Calories: 40, Fat: 0.2g, Carbs: 10g, Protein: 0.5g, Sugar: 6g, Sodium: 3 mg, Potassium: 60 mg, Cholesterol: 0 mg

SPICY GINGER ZINGER

Preparation Time: 10 min
Cooking Time: none
Mode of Cooking: No Cooking
Servings: 2
Ingredients:

- 2 inches fresh ginger root, peeled and sliced
- 1 small red chili, deseeded and chopped
- Juice of 2 oranges
- 1 Tbsp honey (omit for Whole30)
- 2 cups ice-cold water
- Fresh basil leaves for garnish

Directions:

1. Juice ginger and red chili using a juicer
2. Combine ginger-chili juice with orange juice and ice-cold water in a pitcher
3. Stir well to mix
4. Serve garnished with fresh basil leaves

Tips:

- Ginger can be juiced ahead and stored in the refrigerator for up to a week
- Increase or decrease red chili based on spice preference
- For Whole30 compliance, omit honey and adjust sweetness by adding more orange juice if needed

Nutritional Values: Calories: 35, Fat: 0.2g, Carbs: 8g, Protein: 0.7g, Sugar: 6g (omit honey for Whole30), Sodium: 4 mg, Potassium: 120 mg, Cholesterol: 0 mg

COCONUT WATER HYDRATOR

Preparation Time: 3 min
Cooking Time: none
Mode of Cooking: No Cooking
Servings: 1
Ingredients:

- 1 cup coconut water
- 1 Tbsp chia seeds
- Juice of 1 lime
- 1 tsp grated fresh turmeric
- Fresh mint leaves for garnish

Directions:

1. Stir chia seeds into coconut water and let sit for 10 minutes until gelatinous
2. Add lime juice and grated turmeric
3. Mix thoroughly

4. Garnish with mint leaves before serving

Tips:

- Chia seeds provide additional hydration and energy boost
- Turmeric adds anti-inflammatory properties
- Ensure chia seeds are well dispersed to avoid clumping

Nutritional Values: Calories: 70, Fat: 1.5g, Carbs: 9g, Protein: 2g, Sugar: 5g, Sodium: 42 mg, Potassium: 200 mg, Cholesterol: 0 mg

Measurement Conversion Table

Volume Measurements

US Measurement	Metric Measurement
1 tsp (tsp)	5 milliliters (ml)
1 tbsp (tbsp)	15 milliliters (ml)
1 fluid ounce (fl oz)	30 milliliters (ml)
1 Cup	240 milliliters (ml)
1 pint (2 Cs)	470 milliliters (ml)
1 quart (4 Cs)	0.95 liters (L)
1 gallon (16 Cs)	3.8 liters (L)

Weight Measurements

US Measurement	Metric Measurement
1 ounce (oz)	28 grams (g)
1 pound (lb)	450 grams (g)
1 pound (lb)	0.45 kilograms (kg)

Length Measurements

US Measurement	Metric Measurement
1 inch (in)	2.54 centimeters (cm)
1 foot (ft)	30.48 centimeters (cm)
1 foot (ft)	0.3048 meters (m)
1 yard (yd)	0.9144 meters (m)

Temperature Conversions

Fahrenheit (°F)	Celsius (°C)
32°F	0°C
212°F	100°C
Formula: (°F - 32) x 0.5556 = °C	Formula: (°C x 1.8) + 32 = °F

Oven Temperature Conversions

US Oven Term	Fahrenheit (°F)	Celsius (°C)
Very Slow	250°F	120°C
Slow	300-325°F	150-165°C
Moderate	350-375°F	175-190°C
Moderately Hot	400°F	200°C
Hot	425-450°F	220-230°C
Very Hot	475-500°F	245-260°C

CHAPTER 13: 30-DAY MEAL PLAN

WEEK 1	breakfast	snack	lunch	snack	dinner
Monday	Sunrise Sweet Potato and Kale Hash	Handful of mixed nuts	Smoked Salmon and Avocado Citrus Salad	Handful of sunflower seeds	Grass-Fed Beef and Sweet Potato Skillet
Tuesday	Coconut-Cashew Breakfast Skillet	Sliced bell peppers with guacamole	Warm Spiced Beetroot Salad with Pecans	Mixed fruit salad	Pulled Pork with Smoky Dry Rub
Wednesday	Avocado and Tomato Omelet	Apple slices with almond butter	Thyme-Roasted Carrot Ribbon Salad with Almonds	Cherry tomatoes with balsamic	Citrus Zested Chicken with Fennel
Thursday	Spiced Pumpkin and Almond Butter Smoothie	Carrot sticks with tahini dip	Crispy Kale and Apple Salad with Walnut Vinaigrette	Olives and pickles	Lemon Dill Salmon Skewers
Friday	Savory Mushroom and Herb Frittata	Sliced cucumber with sea salt	Spicy Shrimp and Cucumber Salad	Handful of dried apricots	Spicy Tomato and Eggplant Stew
Saturday	Coconut Cinnamon Celeriac Muffins	Handful of berries	Spiced Kale and Apple Salad	Coconut flakes and almonds	Herbed Lemon Garlic Game Hens
Sunday	Avocado Lime Shrimp Salad	Sliced radishes with olive oil	Roasted Beet and Citrus Salad	Celery sticks with almond butter	Spicy Chicken and Kale Soup

WEEK 2	breakfast	snack	lunch	snack	dinner
Monday	Paleo Plantain Pancakes	Sliced carrots with hummus	Avocado and Shrimp Ceviche Salad	Handful of raisins	Herbed Chicken Drumsticks with Cauliflower Rice
Tuesday	Green Plantain Breakfast Hash	Handful of walnuts	Mediterranean Tomato and Cucumber Salad	Sliced cucumber with sea salt	Spicy Pork Stir-Fry with Bok Choy
Wednesday	Sunrise Citrus Salad	Fresh orange slices	Spicy Thai Mango Salad with Cashews	Handful of dried apricots	Lemon-Herb Chicken and Spinach Soup
Thursday	Savory Breakfast Muffins	Celery sticks with almond butter	Warm Spiced Beetroot Salad with Pecans	Mixed fruit salad	Beef and Butternut Squash Chili
Friday	Coconut-Cashew Breakfast Skillet	Handful of mixed nuts	Smoked Salmon and Avocado Citrus Salad	Cherry tomatoes with balsamic	Spicy Coconut Shrimp Stew
Saturday	Avocado and Tomato Omelet	Apple slices with almond butter	Thyme-Roasted Carrot Ribbon Salad with Almonds	Olives and pickles	Mediterranean Fish and Vegetable Soup
Sunday	Spiced Pumpkin and Almond Butter Smoothie	Sliced bell peppers with guacamole	Crispy Kale and Apple Salad with Walnut Vinaigrette	Handful of sunflower seeds	Rustic Beef and Root Vegetable Stew

WEEK 3	breakfast	snack	lunch	snack	dinner
Monday	Smoked Salmon and Asparagus Frittata	Handful of berries	Spiced Kale and Apple Salad	Mixed fruit salad	Spicy Tomato and Eggplant Stew
Tuesday	Sunrise Sweet Potato and Kale Hash	Sliced radishes with olive oil	Roasted Beet and Citrus Salad	Cherry tomatoes with balsamic	Lemon-Thyme Roasted Duck
Wednesday	Coconut Cinnamon Celeriac Muffins	Carrot sticks with tahini dip	Avocado and Shrimp Ceviche Salad	Olives and pickles	Herbed Halibut Packets
Thursday	Paleo Plantain Pancakes	Apple slices with almond butter	Mediterranean Tomato and Cucumber Salad	Handful of dried apricots	Grass-Fed Beef and Sweet Potato Skillet
Friday	Green Plantain Breakfast Hash	Sliced cucumber with sea salt	Spicy Thai Mango Salad with Cashews	Handful of sunflower seeds	Pulled Pork with Smoky Dry Rub
Saturday	Sunrise Citrus Salad	Handful of mixed nuts	Warm Spiced Beetroot Salad with Pecans	Sliced cucumber with sea salt	Citrus Zested Chicken with Fennel
Sunday	Savory Mushroom and Herb Frittata	Sliced bell peppers with guacamole	Smoked Salmon and Avocado Citrus Salad	Handful of raisins	Lemon Dill Salmon Skewers

WEEK 4	breakfast	snack	lunch	snack	dinner
Monday	Spiced Pumpkin and Almond Butter Smoothie	Handful of sunflower seeds	Thyme-Roasted Carrot Ribbon Salad with Almonds	Handful of walnuts	Beef and Butternut Squash Chili
Tuesday	Savory Breakfast Muffins	Handful of dried apricots	Crispy Kale and Apple Salad with Walnut Vinaigrette	Sliced bell peppers with guacamole	Herbed Lemon Garlic Game Hens
Wednesday	Paleo Plantain Pancakes	Mixed fruit salad	Spicy Shrimp and Cucumber Salad	Sliced radishes with olive oil	Spicy Chicken and Kale Soup
Thursday	Sunrise Citrus Salad	Cherry tomatoes with balsamic	Spiced Kale and Apple Salad	Carrot sticks with tahini dip	Spicy Coconut Shrimp Stew
Friday	Savory Mushroom and Herb Frittata	Olives and pickles	Roasted Beet and Citrus Salad	Apple slices with almond butter	Mediterranean Fish and Vegetable Soup
Saturday	Coconut-Cashew Breakfast Skillet	Handful of raisins	Avocado and Shrimp Ceviche Salad	Handful of mixed nuts	Rustic Beef and Root Vegetable Stew
Sunday	Avocado and Tomato Omelet	Sliced cucumber with sea salt	Mediterranean Tomato and Cucumber Salad	Handful of berries	Lemon-Herb Chicken and Spinach Soup

CONCLUSION

As we approach the conclusion of our 30-day journey together, embracing the Whole30 diet, it's important to reflect on the transformative experiences and insights gained. This path isn't just about recipes or temporary changes; it's about laying a foundation for a lifetime of health and vitality. The Whole30 diet, as we've explored, is designed to reset your eating habits, helping you to identify foods that nourish your body optimally and those that don't.

You've learned to scrutinize labels, to cook meals that are as nutritious as they are delicious, and to plan your food intake meticulously. But what happens after these 30 days? How do you maintain the momentum and integrate these habits for the long haul? This is where the true challenge - and reward - lies.

Embracing a whole food lifestyle beyond the structured confines of the Whole30 program involves carrying forward the principles that have started to feel like second nature. You've seen firsthand how the foods you eat affect your energy levels, mood, and overall health. This newfound awareness is a powerful tool in your wellness arsenal.

Looking ahead, the key is to continue honoring your body's needs. This might mean sticking closely to the Whole30 principles, or perhaps you'll find a balance that includes some of your favorite foods, reintroduced cautiously and consciously. Remember, the end of the 30 days is not the end of your health journey; it's the beginning of a mindful eating practice that acknowledges the impacts of dietary choices on both body and mind.

Let's speak realistically about challenges. It's likely that at some point, the motivation that has fueled you might wane, or life's unpredictability could throw your plans off course. Here's where the community, whether online or in person, can play a pivotal role. Surround yourself with support—family, friends, or fellow Whole30 alumni—who understand and respect your food choices and can offer encouragement when it's most needed.

Furthermore, continue to set manageable goals. These don't have to be monumental. Small, daily objectives like incorporating a new vegetable into your meals each week, or planning your food prep days around your schedule, can cumulatively lead to substantial health benefits. Celebrate these little victories—they are stepping stones to sustained change.

Additionally, developing a non-punitive mindset is crucial. If you find you've strayed from the Whole30 guidelines, rather than spiraling into guilt, use it as a learning experience. Analyze what led to that choice and how you felt afterward. This isn't about perfection; it's about progress and learning to make choices that align more closely with your health goals each day.

Throughout this book, we've not only covered the 'hows' but also the 'whys,' providing you with a deep understanding of why certain foods are encouraged and others are eliminated on this diet. This knowledge gives you the freedom to adapt Whole30 principles in a way that fits your individual lifestyle and dietary needs beyond the initial 30 days.

As you move forward, keep exploring and educating yourself on the science of food and its effects on the body. Knowledge is empowering—it enables you to make informed decisions that can dramatically influence your well-being. Websites, podcasts, and books abound with information that can continue to inspire and guide you.

Let's also talk about reintroduction, an aspect we touched on briefly but is worth reiterating. After the 30 days, reintroducing non-Whole30 foods gradually will help you identify any adverse reactions and understand how these foods impact your body. This slow and methodical approach ensures that the efforts of the past month are built upon, rather than undone.

Lastly, remember that the ultimate goal of adopting a diet like Whole30 is not just to change what you eat, but to transform your relationship with food. It's about making conscious food choices, understanding the impact of those choices, and recognizing that you have the power to affect your health positively through diet.

You embarked on this Whole30 journey seeking a reboot—a chance to reset your health and habits. By now, it's hoped that the program has instilled in you a sense of how deeply food is connected to all aspects of your well-being. As you continue making these informed choices, let them be guided not just by dietary rules, but by a deep-seated recognition of what makes you feel your best—strong, clear-headed, and vibrant.

The journey might have begun with a single step taken 30 days ago, but the path continues, winding through life's ups and downs, guided by the principles you've now mastered. Here's to walking that path with confidence, curiosity, and a commitment to your ongoing health and vitality.

Made in United States
Cleveland, OH
27 February 2025

14730663R00066